Frank H. Taylor

Cyclers' and Drivers' Best Routes in and Around Philadelphia

Frank H. Taylor

Cyclers' and Drivers' Best Routes in and Around Philadelphia

ISBN/EAN: 9783744791601

Printed in Europe, USA, Canada, Australia, Japan

Cover: Foto ©Andreas Hilbeck / pixelio.de

More available books at **www.hansebooks.com**

CYCLERS'
AND DRIVERS'

Best Routes

in and around

PHILADELPHIA

With Maps and Illustrations

··1896··

New Wooden....

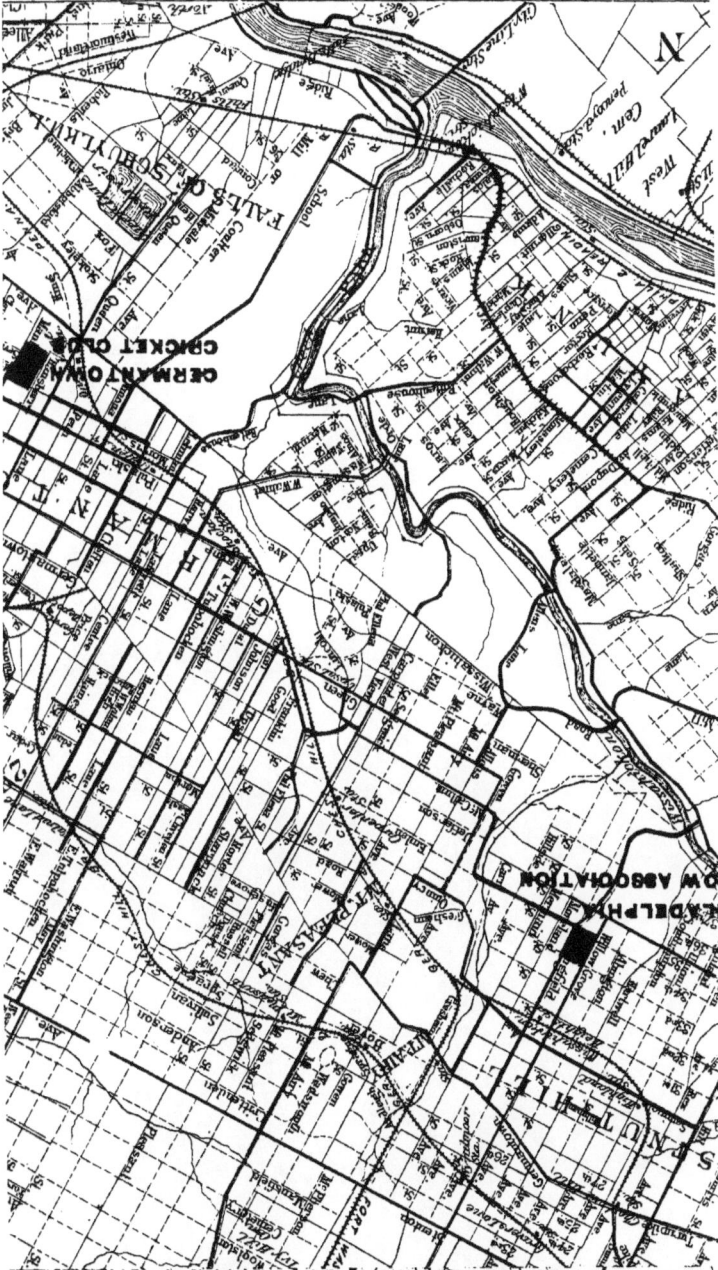

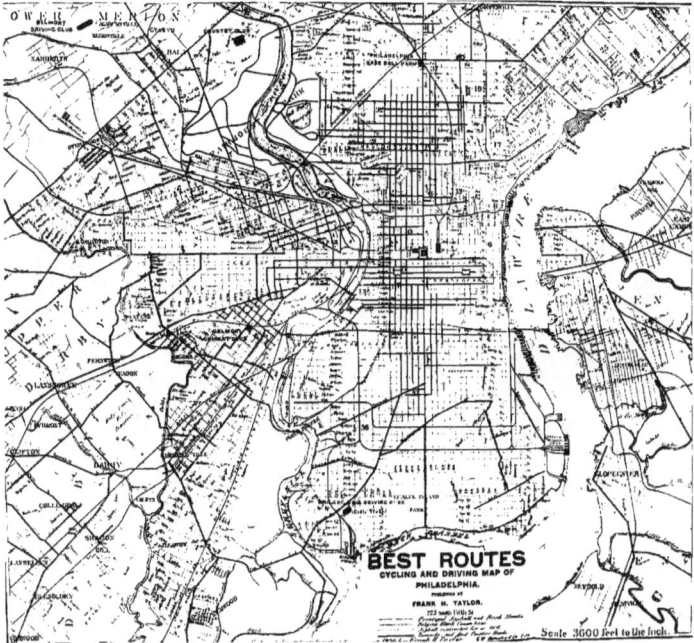

BEST ROUTES
CYCLING AND DRIVING MAP OF
PHILADELPHIA.

FRANK H. TAYLOR.

Scale 3600 feet to the inch.

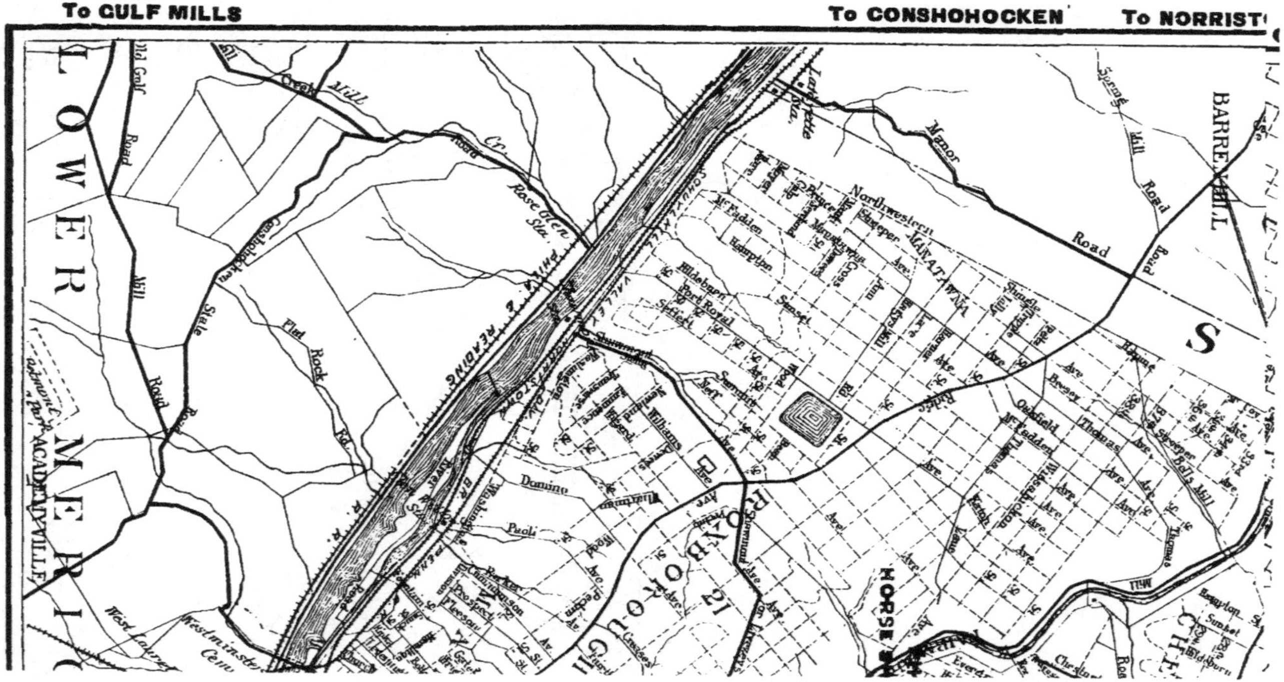

To GULF MILLS
To CONSHOHOCKEN
To NORRIST
LOWER MERION
ACADEMYVILLE
Old Gulf Road
Mill Road
State Road
Flat Rock Rd.
Rose Glen Sta.
Lafayette Sta.
Manor Road
Spring Mill Road
BARREN HILL
MANATAWNA
Northwestern
Domino
Paoli
ROXBOROUGH
21
HORSE
S

New Wooden....
——Cycle Track

OF THE

PHILADELPHIA
)RIVING PARK ASSOCIATION

....AND....

POINT BREEZE BICYCLE
CLUB

ituate on the grounds of the Philadelphia Driving
Park Association, Penrose Ferry Road and
Wheatsheaf Lane.

---

he finest and only track of the kind in the United
States; similar to, but embracing many improve-
ments on, the celebrated cycle track at Montreal,
Canada.

Membership Tickets

ave been issued entitling the holder to the free use of the
Track at all times and free admission to all Bicycle events
during the year 1896, for the small sum of FIVE DOLLARS.
For sale at the office of the Association, No. 914 South Broad
Street, or at the Club House on the grounds.

IATTHEW VOLLMER,	JOS. A. WENDEROTH,
Secretary.	President.
VALTER W. BELL,	THOMAS B. LOVATT,
Assistant Secretary.	Vice-President.

CHAS. A. YOUNG, Treasurer.

or Illustration of Track and Description, see pages 12 and 14.

CYCLERS' AND DRIVERS'

₃est Routes

IN AND AROUND

PHILADELPHIA.

WITH MAPS AND ILLUSTRATIONS.

PRICE, 50 CENTS.

WRITTEN AND ILLUSTRATED BY

FRANK H. TAYLOR,

225 SOUTH FIFTH STREET,

PHILADELPHIA.

1896.

A PRACTICAL GUIDE.

The purpose of this book is to supply the cycling and driving pub!
with information, in compact form, relating to the numerous good stree
and roads leading from the city of Philadelphia into the beautiful regio
around us; to the improved highways threading nearby townships, a1
by directing attention to the many short excursions which may be ma
by wheel or carriage within a few miles of the city, to stimulate the love
exploration through our charming suburbs, which yields to the true cycl
or driver the highest pleasure.

Readers will confer a favor by calling the attention of the author
any omissions or errors that may be discovered.

Disconnected and short sections of asphalt are not shown upon t
maps.

ACKNOWLEDGMENTS.

The publisher is indebted for valuable aid in the preparation of t!
book to many fellow-wheelmen, including the local officials of the L. A. V
whose hearty endorsement of its purpose has been promptly given, a
especial thanks are due to Mr. A. Estoclet, late cycling editor of the *C*
and now of the *Evening Telegraph*, to whose accurate knowledge of rou
is due some of the most attractive features of the work.

.

CITY LINE TOLL GATE, LANCASTER PIKE.

OUT LANCASTER PIKE.

From the earliest days of cycling hereabout, nearly two decades ago, Lancaster Pike has been dear to the wheelman's heart. Its sinuosities, stiff hills and exhilarating coasts recall to all riders of the old-time "ordinarys" a great volume of happy memories. It is still one of the most favored outlets from the urban into the rural districts. Environed by a succession of splendid country seats and dotted by lovely settlements of cottage homes along the main line of the Pennsylvania Railroad, it is the pride of the local rider who loves to pilot stranger wheelmen along its beautiful miles. Lancaster Turnpike extends sixty-seven miles, and is the oldest road of this class in the United States.

The initial point may best be reached by a straight run out Lancaster Avenue, the last mile of which is Belgian, or by passing from Elm Avenue in the Park along the drive around the Catholic Fountain out upon Fifty-second Street and under the railroad bridge.

From the centre of the city one of the prettiest routes now available is out Chestnut Street to Forty-second, to Market Street, new asphalt to Sixty-third and Arch, then take to Sixty-fourth Street for three blocks, to avoid cobbles, and back upon Sixty-third Street, with a fine spin over the hill straight to Overbrook. At Overbrook one is tempted to indulge in a side run among the serpentine avenues of this charming new suburb.

City Line Road, with its pretty little church and its cottage toll-house, is just beyond Overbrook, and then it is a mile and a half to Ardmore, where, just opposite the toll gate, the jolly little country house of the Philadelphia Cycle and Field Club is located, and lucky are you if you know any of the fellows who

THE RED LION, ARDMORE.

3

"live there" on Sundays. Further on is the old "Red Lion" Hotel, wearing prosperous look since cycling grew fashionable, and a little further Haverford College grounds, and the other side of the railroad the grounds of the Merion Cricket Club, whose fine club house will soon replace the one burned in December last.

Merion was described over two hundred years ago (1694) by Gabriel Thomas as a "country village." Bryn Mawr was named in 1683 by Rowland Ellis, a Quaker preacher, after his native place at Dolgelly, Merionithshire. From Bryn Mawr, the abode of wealth and fashion, a fine run crosses Mill Creek and the fertile hills to Conshohocken and Norristown.

At Bryn Mawr the rider may choose either the left or Spring Mill Road via Radnorville, or keep on the pike proper past the Augustinian College of Villa Nova. The roads are reunited at the Spread Eagle Tavern at the upper end of Wayne. Near Centreville, is a block of granite by the roadside indicating the place, six hundred yards distant, occupied by Gen. Anthony Wayne as headquarters. At the old St. David's Church, Radnor, this hero's bones are buried. The Wayne homestead, near Paoli, was built half a century prior to the Revolution, and is still in good repair. Near Malvern Station, also, is the monument commemorating the historic Paoli massacre of September 16, 1777, one of the most dastardly acts of the British troops in that war.

Many of the incidents in T. Buchanan Read's stirring tale, "The Waggoner of the Alleghanies," have this fine old highway as their scene of action. This was, in the early days, called the "Old Conestoga Road." It was the first great highway to the West, and for half a century prior to the opening of the railroad through to Columbia it was crowded with the traffic of "road waggons" and stages. The former carried the ever-increasing freightage to and fro, while rival lines of stages competed for passenger travel. A regular stage left the "King of Prussia," upon High Street, above Third, daily for Lancaster in 1785. The original route was via the present Montgomery Pike, but in 1794 the new turnpike company altered the course of the road to its present location. The turnpike developed a great traffic.

From this time the road-houses multiplied, and through Chester County they were upon the average but a mile apart. Those which became relay-houses, where horses were changed and passengers took their meals, were the envy of their less fortunate rivals between points. Those were indeed lively days in the early decades of the present century.

LANCASTER AND MONTGOMERY PIKES.
(Distances given from City Hall.)

It was necessary to not only care for the hungry passengers, but for the more numerous and voracious wagoners, as well as their horses. The capacity of an inn was gauged by its "horse power," as it were—its room to shelter and feed the animals dragging thousands of heavy Conestoga wagons to and from the city. The driver carried their own bedding and often slept upon the bar-room floor. Some tavern

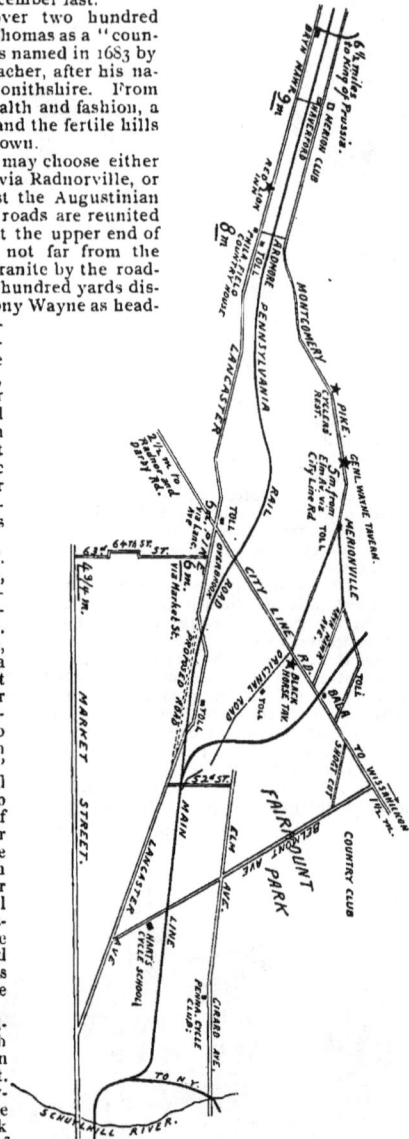

PHILADELPHIA CYCLE AND FIELD CLUB'S HOUSE, ARDMORE.

re exclusively "wagon-houses." The best inns became the centre of local affairs, litical meetings, shows, trainings, vendues, dances, weddings, courts and devonal services (sometimes) were held beneath their broad gambrel roofs.

In 1825 James Reeside, who was a prominent stage owner, introduced gorgeously-inted Troy coaches fitted with steel springs. These were probably among those nich started daily at 7 A. M. from the "Red Lion," at 200 Market Street, and in ese swift, palatial vehicles the public recognized the *ultima thule* of modern travel. e mellow note of the horn, warning the hostlers and the kitchen maids to bestir emselves, was the synonym of the most important haste. And so the Lancaster ke prospered and its little cross-roads settlements, some of them, like Bryn Mawr d Merion, settled long aforetime by hardy Scots, some by the Swedish pioneers, ew into trading centres for the farm people roundabout. Villages hereabout, as on the other roads from the city, took their names from the gay signs of the inns.

In 1834 the first train came through from Columbia, and from that time the de-dence of the busy turnpike began.

MONTGOMERY PIKE.

For the rider who has gained City Line Avenue after the long pull up Belmont venue, through the park, Montgomery Pike offers the shortest route to Ardmore, yond which it keeps parallel with the Pennsylvania Railroad and Lancaster Pike o miles, deflecting here and ending nine miles from its beginning at Gulf Mills, ere meeting the Gulf Road to the "King of Prussia" Tavern and Valley Forge. ce Valley Forge.)

Montgomery Pike is met half a mile or less west of Bala Station, upon City Line venue. At Merionville a quaint little structure of a toll-house (shown in the illustra-on) guards the three roads here converging. At Libertyville the old General Wayne otel still affords "entertainment for man or beast," not to mention myriad cyclers, d divides antiquarian honors with the old Friends' Meeting-house, which also dates way back."

The "Cyclers' Rest," at Libertyville, is a neat little place, much patronized by preciative wheelmen. Half a mile beyond is the Jones House, built by Robt. wens in 1695. Beyond Ardmore the Montgomery Pike passes Bryn Mawr and Rose-ont, all the country round about being beautiful with fine homes and pleasant ts of shade.

TO VALLEY FORGE—A DAY WITH HISTORY.

To Mr. Estoclet (in the *Call*) the writer is indebted for an introduction to the ry interesting tour to and from Valley Forge, over a route measuring forty-four iles.

It leads out Lancaster Pike to Berwin (see Lancaster Pike), where we cross the ilroad at the station, taking the fine turnpike just to the left, and then to the right wn Cassatt's Hill, halting to admire the view, and just beyond the crossing of the hester Valley R. R., as Chesterford stock farm is approached, turn right and down e hill to a brook and a sign, "Valley Forge, two miles;" here turn left and at a ile cross East Valley Creek, the stream of Valley Forge. The road keeps along the ght bank of the creek to the Schuylkill, where the historic Washington Headquar-rs stands. The remains of the winter encampment of the Continental troops are

5

TOLL-HOUSE AT MERIONVILLE, MONTGOMERY PIKE.

found in the woods and upon the hill. Extended embankments and the mound form
ing Fort Huntington are still well defined. Every rocky path and acre of soil i
eloquent with the story of the patriots who suffered here in the long bleak winte
of 1777–8, while the British army made themselves comfortable in the snug houses o
Philadelphia.

It is a pleasant run of two miles down the river side to Port Kennedy; here tun
right up the hill and over the fine Gulf Road to the "King of Prussia" Tavern, dat
ing back to 1769. The time may be much earlier, as the title papers are dated 1718
This famous hostelry was originally kept by a Prussian, who named it in honor o
his monarch. In the time of the Revolution it was a rendezvous for the spies from
the royal army, who came here to get information regarding the patriot army. Th
kitchen is the only part of the original building left unchanged. The wide fireplac
and old crane are still there. From this point it is nearly three miles to Gulf Mill
a place of interest to the historical student, as the large wayside stone records th
fact that the "main Continental Army" encamped here one week prior to occu
pying Valley Forge. The old "Gulph Mill," built in 1747, was burned within the
past year. Our reliable friend, beautiful Montgomery Pike, welcomes us at Gul
Mills, and, after climbing the hill, over its well-graded miles we spin rapidly home
ward.

WAYS TO NORRISTOWN.

The old route of our "ordinary" days still remains much the most comfortable
Reach Bryn Mawr by either Lancaster or Montgomery Pikes, taking the road to th
right, passing Bryn Mawr Hotel, crossing Gulf Road and meeting Conshohocken
State Road near West Conshohocken. Keep to the left along the cinder road t
Ford Avenue and Front Street, go down Ford Avenue, and keep along the wes
side of the Schuylkill, via Front Street, West Conshohocken, and by the railroa
track to Bridgeport (passing Swedesford and its ancient Swedish church, now on
hundred and thirty-six years old), crossing to Norristown upon the covered bridge
The cycling hotel at Norristown is the "Farmers'."

For the homeward run the rider may take Ridge Pike, past the "Black Horse"
and "Marples," to Barren Hill, and thence by a ride of about one mile to the Wissa
hickon at the city line, and thus through the park home. There are few runs of equa
length in the United States and none in this region giving such a diversified succes
sion of beautiful landscapes as this round trip of an afternoon.

By way of variation and as a highly recommended cure for liver complaint
riders can try the Conshohocken State Road, upon its sinuous, hilly and rock
course, from Cynwyd Station to West Conshohocken. The outlooks from the hilltop
along here are superb.

6

THE "GENERAL WAYNE," MONTGOMERY PIKE.

WEST CHESTER PIKE.

The West Chester Pike is a continuation, westward, of Market Street, across
Delaware County and on to the Chester County seat. Cyclists and drivers, who have
long been in the habit of shunning it, will be interested to hear that it is undergoing
considerable improvement, at least within suburban limits. Since the completion of
the electric railway to Llanerch, seven miles out, much of the road has been re-
surfaced.

Hitherto, Manoa, the only nearby locality along its course frequented by our
clubs, has been reached by way of the Lancaster Pike and Haverford. As to West
Chester itself, the favorite mode of access to it is via the Lancaster Pike as far as
Paoli, and thence southwestward along Goshen Road, which meets the pike outside
the town.

When the whole pike becomes cyclable it will be found hilly and picturesque,
traversing as it does Llanerch, Manoa, Broomall (the Drove Tavern of other days)
and Newtown Square, with the old-time cemetery where Anthony Wayne's mother
is buried.

The distance from the Public Buildings to West Chester, by the pike, is about
twenty-three miles, while, by the circuitous route just referred to, it is twenty-nine.

An interesting feature of the West Chester Pike is the new astronomical observa-
tory station of Pennsylvania University, located about three miles west of Milbourne
Mills.

A fine triangular trip of about seventeen miles may be made by taking the Radnor
Road at Llanerch via Lansdowne to Darby and home via Woodland Avenue.

WOODLAND AVENUE TO DARBY.

From the City Hall run out Walnut to the University Grounds and down
Spruce, which is asphalted to Woodland Cemetery gate, and good Belgian or
macadam to Fifty-eighth Street and Woodland Avenue, which, from this point
to Darby, is paved with brick. The Belgian can be avoided by a preferable
route along Walnut or Spruce to Forty-second Street, to Chester, to Forty-
seventh or Forty-ninth Streets, to Woodland Avenue. The most interesting
features of this pleasant run are the noble group of the Pennsylvania University Buildings, including its new dormitories; Woodland Cemetery, established in 1840 upon the old country seat of Andrew Hamilton. to whom it was
deeded by Penn in 1704; the Episcopal Divinity School at Fiftieth Street;
Bartram's Garden, now one of the city parks, and reached by a brief detour to
the left from Fifty-fourth Street; the old Quaker Church at Sixty-eighth Street;
St. Vincent's Home for Infants; and the Blue Bell Tavern at Paschallville, built
in 1762. Here. upon Cobb's Creek. stood the first grist mill built in the State,
and erected by John Printz, Governor of the Swedish Colony, from whom it was
bought by William Cobb. Opposite the Blue Bell the Island Road leads over
the ridge and the low lands for either Tinicum or Penrose Ferry Bridge.

The Blue Bell Tavern, at Paschallville, preserves its original quaintness.
It was built in part, at least, in 1766.

Paschallville is five miles from City Hall, and it is one mile and a half to

Darby. At Darby the Buttonwood Inn maintains a good restau
inal Buttonwood Inn was built in 1739 by George Wood. 1
many miles, is most attractive for water colorists. From Darby
surmount the hill across the bridge and speed along Chester Pi
Tinicum; or, by choosing Darby and Radnor Road (Lansdow
may return to the city via Lansdowne, Baltimore Pike, throug]

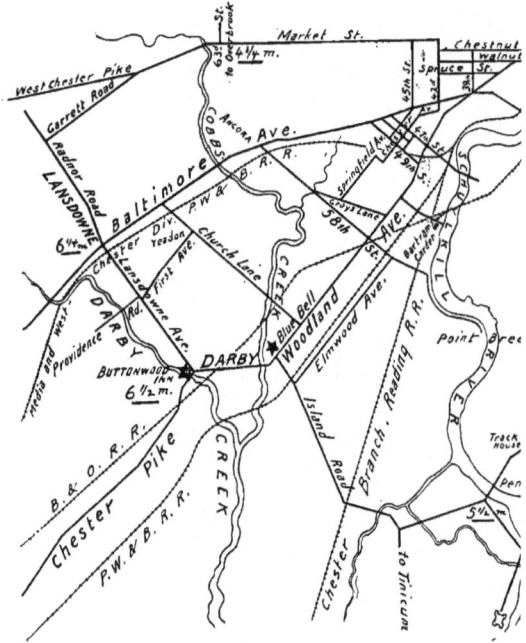

DARBY RIDING DISTRICT.
(Distances given from City Hall.)

8

ngora, and the beautiful neighborhood between Forty-ninth and Forty-fifth reets, all of which is paved with brick.

The best connecting link between Woodland Avenue and Baltimore Avenue Fifty-eighth Street, which is newly telforded to Gray's Lane, and is very fine. short cut may be made from Fifty-eighth Street midway down Gray's Lane. ossing Ameaseka Creek, a very pretty spot, and turning left into Springfield venue, a good dirt road, which, after passing the Belmont Cricket Club grounds, eets the brick at Forty-ninth Street and Chester Avenue. Church Lane, tween Fernwood and Sixty-eighth Streets, crosses a pretty bit of country, but not always in prime order. First Avenue, which springs from Church Lane uthwest at Yeadon, is a thoroughly good run to Lansdowne Avenue.

BRIDGE OVER DARBY CREEK, PROVIDENCE ROAD.

9

"BUTTONWOOD INN," DARBY.

DARBY TO LANSDOWNE AND BEYOND.

Round about Darby was the land of the Okehockings. Darby Creek come from beyond Wayne and Berwyn, gathering the flow of a hundred rivulets and fretted by scores of mill wheels. Every mile has its gem for the artist and it exploration to the source is a delight.

No trolley cars vex the wheelman beyond Darby on the Darby and Radno Road (Lansdowne Avenue). From the Buttonwood Inn to Lansdowne th highway runs nearly parallel with beautiful Darby Creek, and is bordered with pretty homes and not a few costly country seats. The Darby Library, upon th right at the start from Darby, is one of the oldest in the United States. Hal way to Lansdowne First Avenue meets Lansdowne Avenue, and by turning right it will bring the rider past the Holy Cross Cemetery to Church Lane, a Yeadon. A little further along Lansdowne Avenue Providence Road descend steeply on the left to the creek, crossing by a quaint covered bridge. (See illus tration.) After crossing, a little side run up the creek will bring into view th old Garrett mill and its pond.

All of the roads about Lansdowne are well cared for. Continuing along th Radnor Road, after crossing Baltimore Pike, at one mile we meet Marshal Road. Good riding in connection with the cross road leading to Fernwood Cemetery at Baltimore Avenue. The fine mansion upon the hill-top beyond the Marshall Road is the Drexel place. Radnor Road meets West Chester Pike at the pretty new settlement of Llanerch. (See West Chester Pike) Garret Road is a direct run to West Chester Pike Chestnut avenue), and connection with the Market Street asphalt at Sixty-third Street.

FROM DARBY TO CHESTER.

The run to Chester is a continuation of the Darby route, via Woodland Avenue Chester Turnpike is noted for its ridable qualities. This was once the King's Highway, and its milestones are said to have borne the royal arms Later it was called the Great Southern Road. The old stage lines from Indian Queen Tavern, in the city, used this route, stopping for dinner at the "Queen of France" Tavern, seven miles beyond Chester. This is now the home of F. F English, the artist. The long hill beyond the ancient hamlet of Darby trie the beginners and many veteran riders, but the climb is worth the trouble The way is bordered with fine homesteads and pretty villages. In turn we pass

THE "WHITE HORSE," CHESTER PIKE.

iron Hill, Llanwellyn, Glenolden, Norwood. Moores and Ridley
White Horse Tavern stands at the top of the hill just beyond
J. T. Knight, the proprietor, has transformed the old orchard
ummer garden, where lady and gentlemen wheelers may lunch
m Moores a side road, now partly occupied by the trolley line,
to the Lazaretto at Tinicum, where the Quaker City and Phila-
lubs have their pretty club houses, and at "Miller's" or Grif-
heelman may find refreshment.
. Creek was built the first piece of railway track, with the single
: piece at Beacon Hill, Boston, in the United States. It was
Thos. Leiper, from his quarry, in 1810.
gained its name from Ridley, England, one Simcock, a native
aving been a large land holder here. From Ridley a good road
iwarthmore, with return via Baltimore Avenue to the city.
itary Academy is passed to the north of Chester, and the little
.hrough its most attractive portion Asphalt or good Belgian
hird Street, and the route toward Wilmington may thus be con-
easant additional spin of three miles, following the trolley track
ie may reach the quaint old settlement of Marcus Hook, where
ie piers of the winter harbor are located. Chester is the oldest
lvania, having been founded by the Swedes half a century prior
imunity laid out by Penn, sixteen miles further up the river.
merly called "Upland," but was rechristened upon the advent
or of the ancient Roman town in England upon the River Dee.
istries are located at Chester, the most important being the ship-
oach & Sons. A pleasant return to the city may be made from
ner. The L. A. W hotel is the Cambridge. There are several
.urants. No toll is charged south of Chester.

BALTIMORE PIKE.

ks of the trolley cars fill this road to the city line, and the trip
n better begin at Lansdowne, reached via Darby Steep hills,
es, shady glens and pretty country seats vary the passing scen-
arthmore good roads extend across country to Ridley Park,
iangular trip. The Central Division of the Pennsylvania R. R.
with this road all the way down, and one may return from any
is stations conveniently. The L. A. W. hotel, at the fine old-
of Media, is the Charter House. A few miles beyond Media
: of Refuge and the Williamson School, both worth visiting, are

11

NEW CYCLE TRACK AT THE PHILADELPHIA DRIVING PARK, PENROSE AVENUE.

(See description on page 14.)

LOVATT & FOLEY, ARCHITECTS.

0 THE NEW CYCLE TRACK, PENROSE FERRY AND ISLAND ROAD.

Here is one of the prettiest runs you can find around the Quaker City. Follow
le asphalt to its end down Broad Street; turn right, into Moyamensing Avenue, which
|fine riding; then into Penrose Ferry Road, stopping at the Philadelphia Driving
|.rk to see and perhaps try the new plank cycle track (elsewhere described); then
|png between the rich trucking meadows, dotted with queer little homes and clumps
| willows, to and across Penrose Ferry
|idge. It is the most water-colorable place
|: an artist anywhere near the city.

Just over the bridge a road (not very
|od) leads left down the shore to Fort
|ifflin, a little more than a mile distant.
|he fort proper, built of stone, is just above
|e old "mud" fort and is in charge of a
|rgeant of the army. The old fort was the
|ene of a siege in 1777, lasting three weeks
|om September 27th, when it was
|bjected to the combined fire of the
|'itish fleet and a series of heavy
|nd batteries and floats. At the end
| this attack forty survivors were
|le to retreat. The royal
|gates "Augusta" and
|Merlin" were blown up
|d sunk early in the pro-
|edings.

Half a mile from Pen-
|se Bridge, and just
|ove the Kingsley
|odel farm, is the

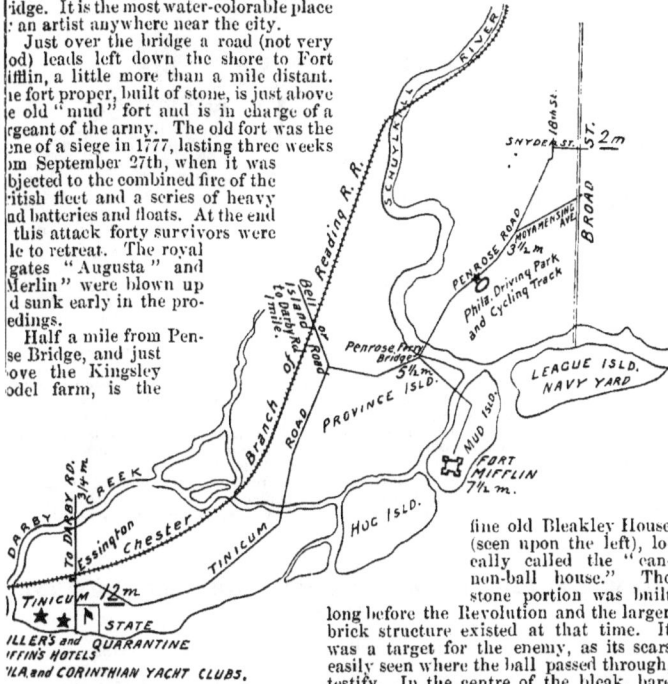

fine old Bleakley House
(seen upon the left), lo-
cally called the "can-
non-ball house." The
stone portion was built
long before the Revolution and the larger
brick structure existed at that time. It
was a target for the enemy, as its scars
easily seen where the ball passed through,
testify. In the centre of the bleak, bare
cornfield is the little family cemetery, sadly
ruined by wandering vandals, where are
buried the nineteen-year-old wife of John
Bleakley and her two little boys, all of
hom died in 1746. John Bleakley was interred beside them twenty-three years later.

The Ferry Road meets Island Road at Suffolk Park, once a popular race track.
rom here the Tinicum Road, generally very ridable, leads down Province Island
id on to the Lazaretto, at Tinicum. (See the Tinicum chapter.) We turn right and
in along the smooth Island Road over the levels and up the ridge, which brings us
'esently face to face with the old "Blue Bell" Tavern, at Paschallville. (See the
Run to Darby.") Returning cityward we may choose to turn right into Elmwood
venue before reaching the Blue Bell. This highway is well telforded to Fifty-
ghth Street, through which two blocks will bring one back to Woodland Avenue
|arby Road).

'ROSE FERRY, ISLAND AND TINI-
CUM ROADS.

Distances given from City Hall.)

OLD CANNON-BALL HOUSE.

13

It is a nice extension of this trip to keep along Fifty - eight h Street and Gray's Lane to Baltimore Avenue, or, for that matter, clear to Market Street, as there is a good cinder path most of the way, with a few dismounts only. While at Fifty-eighth Street and Elmwood Avenue if you wan t a little side diversion coast down to the Schuylkill, pass the oil tanks (don't smoke), and run a mile or more down the dyke to ,Point Breeze. Fine groups of shipping here for photographs. By a little walking the river side may be kept all the way up to Bartram's Garden.

TINICUM (ESSINGTON STATION).

QUAKER CITY AND CORINTHIAN YACHT CLUB HOUSES, AT TINICUM.

Tinicum has great historic interest through the fact that upon this spot was established by Governor John Printz, of Sweden, the first centre of civilized government upon the Delaware River half a century before the coming of Penn. Printz Hall, the governor's residence, is supposed to have stood upon land long since absorbed by the river.

As already indicated (see "Chester Pike") Tinicum may be reached via Darby and Chester Pike by a ride eastward one and a half miles from Moore's. This road has been nearly spoiled by the branch trolley line. It can usually be reached quite as pleasantly by the road leading down from the junction of Island and Penrose Ferry Roads, a pleasant spin along the dykes and meadows, but sometimes muddy.

At Tinicum the State Quarantine establishment is located, but it is of more interest to the fashionable youth of both sexes, who come hither as the headquarters of the Quaker City and Corinthian Yacht Clubs, whose picturesque fleets of sailing and steam yachts, big and little, fill the channel in front. Upon Sundays and regatta days the Tinicum shore is a lively and picturesque place. Now cycling visitors reach Essington Station upon the Chester trains from B. & O. Station at Twenty-fourth and Chestnut Streets.

NEW CYCLE TRACK AT POINT BREEZE DRIVING PARK.

OWNED BY THE PHILADELPHIA DRIVING PARK ASSOCIATION.

In connection with the foregoing tour the following description of the new and costly cycling track above alluded to is in order.

This is the first track built upon this principle in the United States. Its length is seventeen hundred and sixty feet, or one-third of a mile at eighteen inches from the inside pole. It is twenty-six feet six inches wide at the banked ends of the ellipse, twenty-five feet wide on the back-stretch and forty feet wide on the home-stretch. The banks, or curves, are built on a grade of about eighteen degrees. The material used is best Georgia yellow pine, one and a half by two and a half inches, laid on diagonally and keyed in four places.

The back-stretch is four hundred and forty feet long and the home-stretch, between the meeting points of curved ends with the straight run, is three hundred and forty feet to the tape.

The high banks at ends are protected by a rail about two feet high. The track has cost about $10,000 to construct, and is the only wooden track in this country. It was built from plans by and under the supervision of Mr. George I. Lovatt, architect assisted by M. F. X. Foley, consulting engineer.

Upon an official trial, November 27th, 1895, Wm. A. Wentzell, of Philadelphia reduced the Class A record for ten miles by forty seconds, and the following day the same rider, with Lloyd Beverlin, rode an unofficial mile upon a tandem in 1.56 Inquiries regarding this valuable addition to our local cycling attractions should be addressed to H. H. Bell, at the office of the association, 914 South Broad Street, who issues tickets, giving admission to all cycling meets and the use of the track during the year, at the price of five dollars. Tickets may also be bought at the club house.

14

ON THE WISSAHICKON.

THROUGH EAST FAIRMOUNT PARK AND UP THE WISSAHICKON.

The East River Drive, along the Schuylkill River from Lemon Hill to the mouth of the Wissahickon, may be reached best via Spring Garden Street, Girard Avenue, Oxford Street, Columbia Avenue or Diamond Street. By the first-named approach entrance is made into the Park at Green Street; passing the Lincoln Monument, erected in 1871, and the beautiful boat club houses ranged along the shore, upon the left, which in their order are: The Fairmount Rowing Association, Quaker City, Pennsylvania, Crescent, Bachelors', University Barge, Philadelphia, Malta, Vesper, West Philadelphia and Iona Clubs, with the Philadelphia Skating Club and the Humane Society. Notable features of the drive below Girard Avenue Bridge are the "Tam O'Shanter" group of figures opposite the boat clubs and the new Garfield Statue. Half a mile above the tunnel at the Spring Garden Pumping-station, a drive leads under the Reading Railroad and up the hill past the reservoir and connecting with Diamond Street. The way to the Wissahickon keeps close to the river, passing Laurel Hill, Philadelphia's most noted cemetery, and Fall's Village, where "Tissot's" well-known hostelry offers a "kind invite," and where, a little above, the Bachelors' Boat Club country house, the Turf Villa and "Ringstetten," the headquarters of the Undine Barge Club, are seen. Just below the Wissahickon the City Line Bridge (toll) spans the river and forms the link connecting the two splendid wheeling sections to the north and south of the Schuylkill together.

The placid splendor of our peerless Wissahickon is realized at the point of rocks as we enter its shadows and bowl along its lovely roadway. The stream may be followed from Ridge Avenue to the city line, a distance of about seven miles, or twelve miles from the City Hall, of which ten are in Fairmount Park, upon one of the best and most picturesque roads in America. Several quaint little road-houses, of time-honored repute, are maintained along the stream. The first of these is the Riverside at Ridge Avenue; half a mile above, the Maple Shade; one mile, the Wissahickon Hall at the Red Bridge; two miles, Lotus Inn; at Monastery Lane, three miles, the Indian Rock Hotel; and lastly, three and one-half miles, Valley Green, of many pleasant memories.

Beyond the city line the road to the left leads to Barren Hill and Norristown, and to the right toward Flourtown and thence to Fort Washington and Ambler, through White Marsh Valley. Rittenhouse, West Walnut and Springfield Lanes at Valley Green guide the rider up the hills into the riding districts of Germantown.

Gipsy Lane, at the Maple Shade, is a short but steep and unridable way to School Lane. The latter is one of the prettiest of Germantown's drives.

Hermit Lane, indicated upon the map, marks the path to the spot where Johann Kelpius, the Hermit of the Wissahickon, lived two centuries ago. At Rittenhouse Lane the little Cresheim Creek, named after Kriegsheim, Germany, plashes into the Wissahickon, and just here, at the Devil's Pool at the bend, a skirmish occurred during the battle of Germantown between Hessians and Continentals.

15

The beautiful highland, called Wissahickon Heights, to the northeast of the Wissahickon, is noted in connection with the elegant and fashionable Wissahickon Inn, the fine grounds of the Horse Show Association, the club house and field of the Philadelphia Cricket Club and for many costly residences, which have combined to make this one of the most fashionable of suburbs. Wissahickon Heights are reached via the massive stone bridge spanning the creek at Rex Avenue.

The Wissahickon Inn has always been popular and "up to date." Among the improvements of the last and present season is a large room, well lighted, with an instructor for beginners in the sport of cycling. A large swimming pool is one of the attractions. The manager is Mr. W. S. Anderson. Riders to this point may spend an agreeable evening and return to Broad Street Station by rail in less than half an hour.

WEST FAIRMOUNT PARK ROADS AND BY-WAYS.

PARK REGULATIONS.

The three thousand acres of Fairmount Park are threaded with some fifty miles of principal drives and nearly one hundred miles of lanes and by-paths. What an endowment for the Philadelphia cyclist!

The approaches and roads of the eastern part of the park are described elsewhere. (See River Drive and Wissahickon.)

The principal points of ingress to West Fairmount Park are as follows:

1. At Mantua Avenue and Thirty-fourth Street, opposite Fairmount Dam, easily reached from Lancaster Avenue or across Callowhill Street bridge. This leads along the river past Zoo Garden, connecting with Girard Avenue entrance or the West River Drive.
2. At the west end of Girard Avenue bridge.
3. At Fortieth Street and Elm Avenue.
4. At Fifty-second Street and Elm Avenue.
5. Via City Line Bridge from the Germantown district.
6. At New "Falls" bridge at "Falls of Schuylkill."

To define all the combinations of rides possible in this charming maze of picturesque wanderings would involve a book in itself.

The three principal drives are: The New River Road, Lansdowne Drive and Belmont Avenue. Leading away from these, uphill and down, are the by-ways and short-cuts along Centennial Lake, around Horticultural Hall and Memorial Hall, to George's Hill, to Belmont Mansion, to Belmont Pumping-station, to Chamounix and to the Country Club.

The worst piece of road in the Park (and there are many) is the River Drive on the west side, from the Stone Bridge to Girard Avenue. It has long been hopelessly unridable, and will probably continue so.

Park regulations call for a bell, a lantern at night, pace not exceeding seven miles per hour, not more than two abreast, no coasting.

HISTORIC AND OTHER NOTABLE BUILDINGS IN FAIRMOUNT PARK.

The peerless domain of Fairmount Park is made up from a series of noble old estates once the homes of the "fathers of the soil," notable men of wealth and taste, and there is no space in America of equal area so plentifully dotted with historic reminders of other times, courtly men and fair women.

Lemon Hill Mansion stands upon the site of the home of Robert Morris, the patriotic financier of the Revolution, whom an ungrateful people afterwards per-

16

A BY-PATH ALONG THE WISSAHICKON.
(Drawn from a Photograph by Dr. A. Wint.)

mitted to suffer in want and spend years in a debtors' prison to their everlasting disgrace. He called the place "Old Vineyard Hill." In 1796 a Mr. Pratt erected the present structure, and it was known as "Pratt's Garden."

At Sedgeley, just above Lemon Hill, was formerly a porter's lodge for a fine mansion, built for and occupied by Leslie, the famous English artist

Mt. Pleasant (now the popular "Dairy") was built by John McPherson in 1761 whose son, a young officer in the American forces of the British army, resigned and became a distinguished officer of the Revolution.

In 1779 the place was bought by Benedict Arnold, prior to his treason, and hither he brought his bride, the beautiful Peggy Shippen. After its confiscation by the government it was acquired by Baron Steuben, of Revolutionary fame and once a staff officer of Frederick the Great. To him was due the discipline of the Continental army. He died in the seclusion of the wilderness to the north of Utica, N. Y. and is buried there.

Rockland Mansion, now used as a guard-house, stands upon what was once the Edgeley estate, acquired by Wm. Orian, a blacksmith, in 1698, from Wm. Penn.

Strawberry Mansion, well known as a restaurant, was the home of the Swanson family, whose advent long antedated that of Wm. Penn upon this continent.

Solitude, the fine old house in the Zoo Garden, was the homestead of John Penn the poet (a grandson of the founder), who built it in 1785. The transfer of Solitude to the city in 1852 disposed of the last item of property held by the Penn family in America.

"Penn's House," the little brick home of the founder, was brought from Letitia Street (named for his daughter) and set up close by Girard Avenue not many year ago.

Sweetbriar Mansion, the restaurant upon Lansdowne Drive, was built in 1791 by a Mr. Ross, and afterward occupied by Samuel Brock, author of the bill for the establishment of the common school system of the State.

Belmont Mansion is the most notable of the park buildings. It was erected here in 1745 by Wm. Peters. The owner remained a loyalist during the Revolutionary War, and early in the struggle went to England and ended his days there. His son Richard Peters, was a patriot, and during the war was Secretary of the Board of War later a member of Congress, and for nearly forty years a judge of the United States District Court. He was renowned for hospitality, and the best song (grave or gay) was a noted wit, and, in all, the most genial and desirable company. The Chevalier de la Luzerne, Benjamin Franklin, Christian Samuel, Rittenhouse the astronomer Bartram, Wharton, the Baron de Steuben, Inspector-General of the American Army during the Revolution, Tallyrand, Louis Philippe, Robert Morris, the Count de Survilliers, John Penn the governor, Alex. J. Dallas the advocate, John Adams, Jefferson and Washington, were all frequent and welcome guests. On the south front few years ago stood a chestnut tree planted by Washington, the hole being dug by the general with Judge Peters' cane. Two thrifty chestnuts, the offspring of the one planted by Washington, still stand near the site of the parent stock. A white walnut planted by Lafayette during his visit in 1824, stands close by. The large apartmen in the rear was first used to entertain the Duke Alexis, of Russia. Close by the hous is the head of the ditch once used for the inclined railway, forming a part of the firs rail line to the West.

Old Landsdowne Mansion, built by John Penn, stood upon the site of Horticul tural Hall, and was the refuge of Joseph Bonaparte, King of Spain, after Waterloo

The little house by the shore of the river, called "Tom Moore's Cottage," gain its name from the fact of his allusion to it in one of his poems.

"Chamounix" is the place once called Mt. Prospect, erected by George Plum sted, merchant, in 1802. It is the most remote and least-visited place in the entir park, but the surroundings are extremely picturesque.

Of the modern structures in the park, the massive Memorial Hall with its super free museum, Horticultural Hall, the English Commission Buildings and the Ohi Buildings, are reminders of the Centennial. There are none others of note.

During the summer excellent bands give concerts in pavilions at Lemon Hill Strawberry Mansion and Belmont Mansion in the afternoons.

THE FRANKFORD, HOLMESBURG AND TORRESDALE RIDING DISTRICT.

As yet Frankford enjoys no ideal cycling connection with the interior city. The ride across town, via the Girard Avenue asphalt, ends in a *cul de sac* of hopele cobbles near Port Richmond. Frankford wheelmen come and go via Lehigh Avenue from Broad Street eastward, upon asphalt to Sixth Street, Belgian to Fifth Stree same up Fifth to Glenwood Avenue, along the latter to the right, and up Old Secon Street to Nicetown Lane, which brings riders to the Arrott Street asphalt and over to Frankford Avenue. The shortest and most reliable route throughout all season is via Lehigh Avenue to Kensington Avenue and up that busy thoroughfare direct to Frankford. It involves a long stretch about two and a half miles of good Belgia block, considerable of which may be avoided by side paths. From the entrance int Frankford the asphalt extends up Main Street (or Frankford Avenue) nearly a mil Thence to the foot of the hill at the junction of Bustleton Pike, the surface is rathe poor Belgian. At this point (Kiggins' Hotel) Bridge Street, newly paved with Be gian, leads east to Tacony Road and the Bridesburg Arsenal. An alternative rou used by some riders takes Erie Street eastward from Broad (soon to be asphalted) a

BUSTLETON

To Wissahickon or Somerton

Welsh

BUSTLETON BRANCH

Road

PENNYPACK CREEK

Red Lion H.

POQUESSING CR.

To Bristol

TORRESDALE STA.

Pearson St.

MORELTON INN. STEAMBOAT LDG.

Cottman St. (Township Line Rd.)

Gen. Wayne H.

TO NEW YORK ROAD

Washington H.

Green Tree H.

Rhawn St.

Bustleton Pike.

FRANKFORD AND BRISTOL PIKE

HOLMESBURG JUNC.

R. R.

TACONY R. R.

Longshore St.

Kiggen's H.

TACONY STA.

DELAWARE RIVER

lly Post H.

PENNSYLVANIA

BRIDESBURG STA. U.S. ARSENAL.

'ORD

FRANKFORD CR. Bridge St.

STEAMBOAT LDC.

THE FRANKFORD, HOLMESBURG AND TORRESDALE RIDING DISTRICT.

SPECIAL NOTE.—Since completion of this map Bridge Street has been Bel-
blocked from Kiggins' Hotel eastward, and Cottman Street (Township Line
d) is reported as being perfected west of Oxford Pike.

19

THE JOLLY POST, FRANKFORD.

far as the Newtown Branch of the North Penn Railroad, and along the railroad track
northeast to Nicetown Lane. The Frankford wheelmen have a hospitable club house
at Allen and Main Streets (Frankford Road). At the "Jolly Post," upon Main Street
near Orthodox, or at Kiggins' Hotel, at the junction of Bustleton Pike and Main
Street, good dinners or lunches may be had. The building date of the "Jolly Post"
is unknown, but in 1768 it was advertised for sale. Having, in its time, changed
hands often, it was finally bought by its present owner, Edwin Forrest Smith. After
standing idle for twenty years it was rehabilitated, enlarged and once more became a
popular stopping-place. In 1815 a young officer, Lieut. Richard Smith, shot Capt.
John Carson at this house, the motive being jealousy. Through Frankford several
blocks of Main Street (Frankford Road) are asphalted. Beyond it is Belgian and
macadam.

The favorable location of Kiggins' Hotel, opposite the end of Bridge Street and
at the initial point of Bustleton Pike, together with its excellent reputation, makes it

KIGGINS' HOTEL, FRANKFORD.

MORRELTON INN, TORRESDALE.

opular halting-place. It is conducted by Mr. John F. Kiggins. At the foot of
dge Street the Delaware River steamers stop both ways. Thus a rider from down
n may quickly and pleasantly reach or return from the beautiful runs from Brides-
g up the river. Tacony Road may be reached also from Frankford Road by tak-
Longshore Street. Tacony Road, with its new telfording, cinder side path and
el reaches, is a good route to Torresdale. Morrelton Inn and the beautiful summer
nes hereabout are famous. Morrelton Inn occupies the site of the old Risden's
rry Hotel, the principal structure having been adapted from a fine brown-stone
nsion, once the residence of Edwin M. Hopkins. The main structure is surrounded
a number of handsome buildings belonging to the hotel company, including a
ino, club house, riverside cottage annex, new annex and lawn cottages. The mana-
now in charge of Morrelton Inn is Mr. Harry A. Chester. In the immediate
inity are the country seats of Col. Edw. Morrell, Josiah Bacon, Geo. Carson, Thos.
lan, Nelson Brown, William Fisher, Alexander Brown, Senator Porter, Jesse
ith and other well-known men. Within a short distance are the Morrelton stock
m and track. Steamers reach the city from Torresdale by a run of fifty minutes.
oad leads up either side of the creek to the Bristol Pike, whereon the "Red Lion"
ocated. The best is across the stream, as it avoids a long hill. Good riding is
ed from this point through to Trenton. Opposite the "Red Lion" the trolley
npany is creating, at its terminus, a picnic ground in the fine grove by the creek.

THE BRISTOL PIKE RUN.

From Frankford the Pike is best known as the Bristol Road. It abounds in
ls but is usually fairly good. The distance to Holmesburg is three and one-half
les, and to Torresdale three miles more. Just below Holmesburg is the beautiful
win Forrest Home for Actors. This place was called "Springbrook," and was
old homestead of the Forrest family. It still contains a wealth of interesting
mentoes of the great tragedian. The superintendent willingly allows entrance to
itors. At Holmesburg are the Washington and Green Tree Hotels, and upon the
, just across the Pennypack ravine, is the "General Wayne," all old-timers and
d-livers. The "Green Tree" was built about the beginning of the present cen-
y. The "General Wayne" has a history dating from 1776, as an old sign, which
merly swung from its post in front, testified. The Washington Hotel is one of the
ly hostelries of this road and existed at a time when the settlement was called

21

EDWIN FORREST HOME FOR
ACTORS, NEAR HOLMESBURG.

FORREST'S
FAVORITE CORNER

Washington. The hotel was long conducted by John Risdon, who had earlier owned the Risdon's Ferry Hotel at Torresdale, and from here he ran a stage line to the city. Later it was managed by John Robinson, Joseph Fell, John Mason, Joseph Hellings and F. C. Michener. Capt. Robert Johnson, the present landlord, took it in 1875. General Washington is said to have attended fox hunts here, and in 1824 Lafayette held a reception at the hotel. For many years it was an important halting-place for the through stages to and from New York. It is now a favorite with the cycling public. A splendid coast may be had down Pierson Avenue from Bristol Pike toward the Tacony or River Road.

The principal roads across country from the Frankford and Bristol Pike are: The

WASHINGTON HOTEL, HOLMESBURG.

THE RED LION, NEAR TORRESDALE.

'ord Pike from Frankford to Fox Chase, poor in places; the Bustleton Pike to
tleton, also rather poor; Cottman Street, or Township Line Road, excellent to
Second Street, but rough beyond; the beautiful Old Welsh Road from Holmes-
g via Bustleton to Bethayres, Huntington Valley, Sorrel Horse and Willow Grove.
'ond Bustleton the Welsh Road is ordinary.

The "Red Lion" Hotel, besides the beautiful Poquessing Creek, near Torresdale,
built in 1730 by Philip Amos, but was given its present name in 1770. In 1781
shington's army camped here en route to Yorktown. August 29, 1774, the Penn-
'ania delegates to the First Continental Congress came out here to the county
to meet and entertain at the "Red Lion" the delegates from Massachusetts.

A round-about but interesting way to reach Holmesburg is via Old York Pike,
cy Road, Old Second Street Pike (very fine) and Cottman Street (Township Line
id). (See chapter on Old Second Street Pike.)

Beyond the Poquessing, through Bensalem Township, the road continues ex-
ent through Bristol. The road is especially attractive at Bristol, passing close
de the river bank, which is bordered by many quaint and elegant homes. The
apike coquettes with the Pennsylvania Railroad all the way to Trenton, and
nighout it presents to the passer by a lovely succession of picturesque features
a as are only found where the fertile uplands and green meadows of the Delaware
e together. The United States Hotel, at Trenton, is cycling headquarters. It is
rally located and among the best known of Jersey hotels. The proprietor is Mr.
n J. McCarthy.

OLD YORK PIKE, THE CHELTENHAM RIDING
DISTRICT AND WILLOW GROVE.

The splendor and dignity of the country life, near our large cities, is nowhere
more completely exhibited than around about Cheltenham Township, upon
ise roads and lanes, which have been favorite drives for generations, seventy
isand dollars have been recently expended. The wheelman who cares to explore
lovely territory, may reach it by a run of fifteen miles.

Old York Road is said to have followed the trace of an Indian trail. It was the
icipal road to New York until the more direct and less hilly route via Frankford
Bristol was made. It has been a turnpike since 1803.

Just below the junction of Broad and Cayuga Streets take the path along the
e to the left, opposite the Hunting Park, once famous as a race track, now a city·
n. Old York Pike is good from Rising Sun Lane. The pike is in superb condi-
. Just beyond the dip of the road into the Wingohocking Valley, once called
ff Mill Hill, is the beautiful old Lovering place on the left (note the Grecian
ch) now owned by J. B. Lippincott, Esq. Just beyond are the Graham green-
ses. At Logan Station there is a pleasant little restaurant, and to the westward,
ig Fisher's Lane, are seen, through the trees, Wakefield (Mrs. Samuel Fox), Little
kefield (George W. Carpenter) and Belfield (W. Redwood Wright). All this sec-

23

tion was a part of " Stenton," the famous estate founded by Logan, secretary of Wm. Penn. The handsome place upon the west side beyond Logan Station (note the hedge) is " Fairfield," built by Alfred Cope (Mrs. Philip C. Garrett). " Woodfield " is next beyond on west side (Col. J. M. Moore). Upon the east side is the Jewish Hospital. Opposite is the residence of Mr. H. Rogers. At Thorp's Lane, upper side, and on the west, is the old Butler place, built by a Frenchman, named Boullange, and bought in 1810 by Major Pierce Butler, a wealthy South Carolinian, of noble English family, whose unhappy marriage with the famous Fanny Kemble is a matter of history. The Scheutzen Park is upon Olney Road, east of the Pike. Clayton's Hotel is at Branchtown, where Mill Street comes in from Germantown. Opposite is the old De Benneville house. At Fern Rock, on west side, is the place of J. S. Lovering Wharton. " The Oaks " was long owned by the late Charles Sharpless. At Green Lane, in the little De Benneville graveyard, are buried General Agnew and Lieut-Colonel Byrd, British officers, who fell at the battle of Germantown. The graves are unmarked. Dr. Wistar's place, on the west side, " Roadside," was once the home of Lucretia Mott.

From Milestown Oak Lane leads to the right to Oak Lane Station and its pretty group of properties. City Line Hotel marks the limit of the city. Beyond are Mr. Frey's, Mr. Shinn's, at the corner of Stenton Avenue, with Mr. Dobbins' opposite (on the right), Mr. Stetson's, Mr. Roeloff's, Mr. Barney's (where Mr. Jay Cooke resides) and Mrs. Loeb's near the station.

It is a pleasant little run from Ogontz Station out the old Pike, turning left on Church Road and left again into Rock Creek Lane, following up the stream behind Ogontz Ladies' Seminary. This is a lovely bit. The Cooke Mausoleum gleams among the verdure across the stream, and for a water colorist the old mill and its pond form a prize. We emerge upon Washington Lane—ride up the hill, to the left, to Chelten Avenue; here is Cheltenham Military Academy and opposite Mr. Cresson's beautiful home.

Down Chelten Avenue, upon the right, is Mr. Weidener's place and at half a mile, the second road, turn right into a winding lane (Serpentine), passing the princely Elkins' place, the way bordered with great cone-like cedars, locally called " The Needles"—this returns us to Old York Pike.

Mr. Wanamaker's place is at Chelten Hills Station, reached via Washington Lane. At Jenkintown the Cottman House welcomes wheelmen. Beyond, the hills are long and

OLD YORK PIKE.
(Distances given from City Hall.)

24

IVY GREEN.
ORIGINAL CHELTENHAM ACADEMY BUILDING

OLD MILL ROCK LANE.

eep, but the road magnificent. All about Jenkintown there are handsome homes
id fine roads.

A favorite objective point upon the Old York Pike is Willow Grove, five miles
:yond Ogontz, where the old hotel, under the vivifying influence of trolley picnics
id wheelmen combined, has become a very lively and delightful place. Non-cycling
embers of wheelmen's families may join them here by the trolley cars, which come
om Walnut Street. The Union Traction Company has just created a fairy land
'fifty acres here, including a pretty lake, rustic lodge, casino, pavilions, an elec-
ic fountain, fitted for prismatic effects; a water chute, cycling track and many
her amusing features. The *Call's* cycling editor has defined a further route from
:re up the Doylestown Turnpike to Doylestown and back to Willow Grove upon
ork Pike, but Willow Grove is far enough and good enough for me.

XFORD PIKE, OR OLD SECOND STREET, TO BETH-
AYRES, SORREL HORSE AND NESHAMINY FALLS.

If you are strictly an asphalt rider don't attempt this trip; it has its vicissi-
des.

The adventurous wheelman who essays it comes home enthusiastic and tries it
:ain.

The way is along Rising Sun Lane through Franklinville to Oxford Pike, cross-
g first Wingohocking Creek and then the larger Tacony Creek (both Indian names,
spectively, "place for planting" and "uncleared wood"). Olney, Crescentville,
iwndale and the Old Oxford Church are on the route. At Fox Chase Inn bear to
e left toward Rockledge and there enter Montgomery County; then push up
allowell Hill, the summit of which is crowned with the fine Craige Lippincott
ansion. A telford road to the left, at this point, leads over to Jenkintown and the
ieltenham riding section—distance two and one-half miles.

At the foot of the hill we cross the Pennypack Creek at Valley Falls, and close
:yond Bethayres Station upon the "Bound Brook" route (Reading R. R.)—a good
ace to rail home from if tired. At Huntington Valley P. O. is the Lady Washing-
n Inn, the oldest upon this route; two miles further reaches the "Sorrel Horse,"
id dinner. After a smoke on the porch we travel upon Byberry Road over to
merton, two and one-half miles; turn left at the hotel and zig zag along the "Trap

OLD BRIDGE WASHINGTON LANE

RES. of HON JOHN WANAMAKER

25

TOLL-HOUSE UPON LIMEKILN PIKE,
ABOVE WASHINGTON LANE.

(From drawing loaned by *The Times*.)

Road " to the Township Line Road, through Prospect Heights, Trevose and Scott's
corner, at signboard, " Bristol eight miles," turning right to Neshaminy Falls.

The home stretch is to Bustleton upon Byberry Pike (crossing Pennypack Creek),
six miles more or less rough ; then three miles to Holmesburg upon the beautiful
Welsh Road. For the rest see " Bristol Pike." Total ride back to City Hall, forty-
four miles.

LIMEKILN PIKE.

Limekiln Pike has its beginning at Mill Street, near Branchtown, upon Old York
Pike. It is to the west and slightly divergent from this old highway, traversing
Cheltenham, Upper Dublin and Horsham Townships. The road crosses the North
Penn Railroad at Edge Hill, ten miles from the City Hall. The advance of the left
wing of the Continental Army at the battle of Germantown was along this old road.
There are hotels at Fitzwatertown and Jarrettown, but many wheelmen make the
old " Three Tons," just beyond Pennville upon the Spring House Road, their objec-
tive point. The Butler Pike leads from here to Ambler.

BETHLEHEM PIKE.

The Bethlehem Pike traverses a section of fruitful Montgomery County, which
early attracted a thrifty population of Swedes, English, French, Scotch, Irish and
Hollanders, the product of whose grain fields was ground at massive mills established upon its abundant water courses. The King's Road, this same turnpike, was
commenced in 1704, and was the great highway between the town of Philadelphia
and the Moravian settlements upon the Lehigh. It was still a rough country road
when Washington's ammunition trains and quartermaster's wagons came jolting
along from Bethlehem, and the crowding wagons of wounded soldiers were conveyed
hither.

In 1802 it became a part of the property of the Germantown and Perkiomen
Turnpike Company, whose route commenced in Second Street, whose original fran-
chise led via Chestnut Hill and the Bethlehem Road, Plymouth Meeting and Perkiomen Stone Bridge.

" Stage waggons " began regular trips through to Bethlehem in 1763, starting from
the " King of Prussia " in Race Street once every week. In later years several op-
position lines were run over the Bethlehem Road, and the frequent taverns did a rat-
tling business. Flourtown, the first point above Chestnut Hill, was the terminus or
halting place of the frequent local stages about 1820. From Flourtown a good road
leads to the right to and beyond Camp Hill. At the Trenton Cut-off Railroad the
Skippack Pike, a continuation of Church Road from Ogontz (on York Pike) crosses
Bethlehem Pike. Just here is the fine old Whitemarsh Church. Beyond the railroad bridge is Fortside Inn, a new and attractive hotel. Half a mile beyond is a tab-
let beside the road upon the right defining the location of Fort Washington, 600 feet

distant upon the hill crest. Here the main part of the American army was camped from October 20th to December 11th, 1777, marching thence to Valley Forge. The substantial house used by General Washington as headquarters is seen to the south of the hill. The hotel at Fort Washington Station has long been a favorite objective point with wheelmen.

The old settlement of Gilkeson's Corners, through which the pike continues, is just to the east of the handsome and thriving village of Ambler. Dr. R. V. Mattison's beautiful home and grounds is to the right and the old Ambler race track upon the left. At Ambler the wheelman may dine at the modern Wyndham Hotel or the Ambler House opposite the station.

Just above Gilkeson's Corners the Butler Pike crosses, leading upon the right over to the hotel at "Three Tons" upon Sumneytown Pike, a road met by Bethlehem Pike at the Spring House. This ancient hostelry is said to have been the oldest tavern, except the "Blue Anchor" in Dock Street, anywhere in the State. The old building still exists, but has just been merged into a modern structure as a residence.

From Spring-house Corner the rider may continue to the left to Gwynned Corners, and from that point the State Road is direct through Centre Square (on Skippack Pike), Washington Square and Springtown (on Reading Pike) to Norristown.

From Norristown Ridge Pike leads homeward via Barren Hill and the upper Wissahickon Drive, which is met at the City Line. The circuit may be much shortened by returning upon the Skippack Pike, which passes Blue Bell, Broad Axe and Valley Green Corners, and continues through Cheltenham district to York Road, or by taking the Reading (or Perkiomen) Pike at Penn Square, through Springtown, Plymouth and Barren Hill to the Wissahickon.

PERKIOMEN AND GERMANTOWN PIKE.

The Germantown and Perkiomen Pike is the now less favored twin sister of the

BETHLEHEM PIKE.
(Distances given from Chestnut Hill.)

27

Ridge Pike. Like it, it starts practically from the centre of the city, being a pro
longation of Germantown Avenue, but after coming so near as almost to converg
with it at Barren Hill, it takes a more northerly course, passes Norritonville to th
north of Norristown, and terminates at Perkiomen Creek, whence the traveler fo
lows the Perkiomen and Reading Pike to the capital of Berks County. This pike
more frequented by the lover of nature than by the average wayfarer awheel. Alor
its course lies the quaint Quaker village of Plymouth Meeting, with its farm ar
meadow lands and its historic souvenirs. There, in a cluster of maples and cedar
stands the home of the late lamented painter, Thos. Hovenden.

RIDGE PIKE.

The stranger is not likely to feel prepossessed right away in favor of the Ridg
Pike on being told that it is a continuation of Ridge Avenue. The poor riding su
face of the latter is unfortunately too familiar, and many who have once followed th
pike into Norristown subsequently give their patronage to the ups and downs of th
Conshohocken route in preference to it.

Still the Ridge Pike has improved of late years, and is far from unpleasant i
fair weather west of Lafayette Post-office, on Barren Hill, at which point it is easil
struck from the city by way of the Wissahickon Drive. Thence it passes throug
Harmanville (where it is crossed at right angles by the Plymouth and Broad Ax
Pike), Marple's (the old Seven Stars Inn), Black Horse and on to Norristown, a fe
miles beyond which it merges, along with the Perkiomen and Germantown Pik
into the Perkiomen and Reading Pike. As indicated in chapter regarding trip
Valley Forge, Ridge Pike may be used as a part of a very enjoyable round trip.

THE SKIPPACK PIKE.

This important up-country road has its beginning, properly speaking, at the For
side Inn upon the Bethlehem Pike, where it branches to the left, keeping parallel, i
a northwesterly direction, with the township lines. For a dozen miles it is as straigl
as the flight of an arrow, but in its upper portion, as it approaches the Skippac
Creek (twenty-five miles air-line measure from the City Hall), it wobbles after th
fashion of Montgomery County roads generally. The Skippack may be reache
from Ogontz (on Old York Pike) via Church Road, which is its southeastern extensio:
or by the Bethlehem Pike from Chestnut Hill. The most direct route is this wa;
Taking Cayuga street from Broad, Wayne to Tulpohocken and Green to Upsal. He:
take the beautiful Pelham Avenue toward Mt. Airy. One is compensated for th
Belgian blocks of Main Street by a halt at the quaint little Mermaid Inn. At Ches
nut Hill Bethlehem Pike leads to the right with a glorious view of Whitemars
Valley. The first rest on this road is at the "Wheel Water Pump." Near he:
Northwestern Avenue comes in from Wissahickon Drive, which is the third route t
the Skippack. At Flourtown the "Black Horse," "Farmers' and Citizen's" an
"Stahlnecker's" hotels all remain in evidence of the old regime of the stage-coac
days. At present no Sunday dinner can be had here. At "Fort Side" fifteen mil:
have been covered.

Skippack Pike is hilly and somewhat uneven. Broad Axe (and its hotel) an
Blue Bell are respectively seventeen and nineteen miles out. From Broad Axe th
Plymouth Road leads to Ambler upon the right and to Plymouth Meeting and Co:
shohocken to the left. Opposite the quaint little meeting-house is the home of th
noted artist, the late Thomas Hovenden. From this corner the return begins via Pe
kiomen Pike to Fountain Hotel at Barren Hill, where the fountain still flows, an
thence down the long hill (very pasty in wet weather) toward the beautiful conver
group and the peerless Wissahickon Drive at the City Line. The round trip back t
the City Hall, via the East Park Drive, figures about thirty-eight miles. Probabl
the most popular meal station on the route is at Farmer Slater's, on the Plymout
Road, near Broad Axe.

NEW JERSEY.

TO WHITE HORSE PIKE AND ATLANTIC CITY.

A series of turnpiked highways radiate from the suburbs of Camden, whicl
when one has once mastered the perils of our Jersey neighbors' interior higl
ways, affords most enjoyable riding.

The White Horse Pike is much used by wheelmen. From the Marke
Street Ferry-house the route is up two cobble blocks on Delaware Avenue t
Cooper Street, bricks on Cooper to Seventh Street, south on Seventh Stree:
passing Haddon Avenue Station and the City Hall. A better way is to take th
ferry to Federal Street, Camden, ride Federal to Third Street, to Third an
Benson Streets, from which it is brick along Benson to Sixth Street; Sixth t
Berkley Street, across railroad track to Haddonfield Pike, turn to right beyon
first toll-house, and there is White Horse Pike. The rider passes Oaklyn
Orston, Haddon Heights and Magnolia—one of the many suburban hamlet

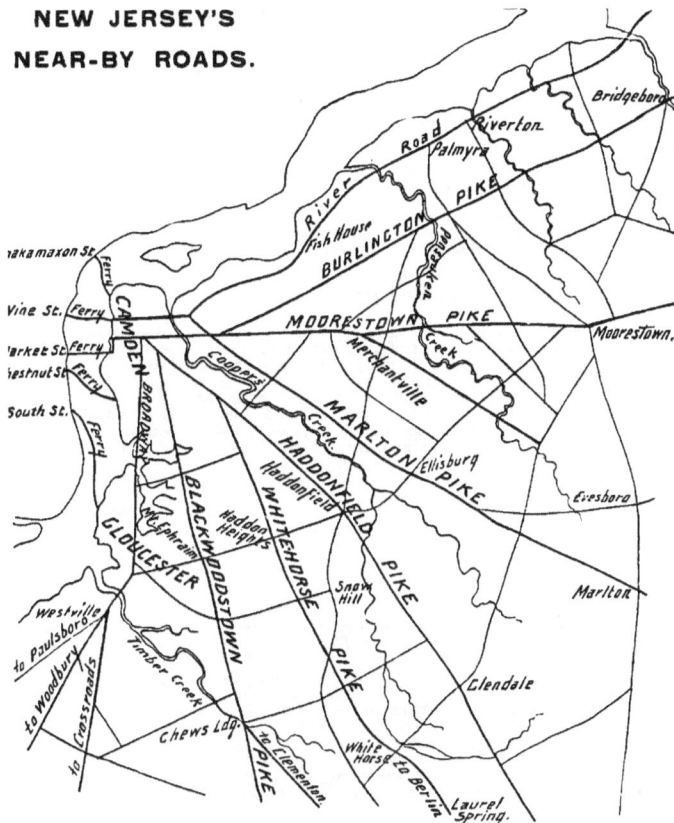

cattered over the world which unconsciously perpetuate the memory of Pierre
Iagnol, the French botanist, born in 1638. Many cottages, plentiful shade and
entle hills vary the route to White Horse Inn, distant from Camden eleven
iiles. The White Horse Inn is about eighty years old and is a picturesque
alting-place. It is conducted by E. B. Davis. To the left of the inn is Lake-
ide, a pretty summer resort. The pike has recently been extended through to
erlin, five miles beyond, and is excellent. Laurel Spring, one mile beyond
ie inn upon the new portion of road, has a good hotel, the Spring House. The
hortest known route to Atlantic City leads this way, via West Berlin, Berlin,
edar Brook, Blue Anchor, Rosedale, Hammonton (dinner). Here take path
long the railroad through DaCosta, Colwell, Woodland, Elwood, Egg Harbor,
rigantine Junction, Farmington and Pleasantville, in all fifty-eight miles.

THE CAPE MAY ROUTE.

A suggestion is made by Mr. Estoclet, in the *Call* series of cycle runs regard-
ig this trip, viz., to start upon Saturday afternoon, stay over night at Millville
hirty-nine miles), at the Weatherby House or the Doughty House, resuming the
ip in the morning, and returning at 3 P. M. to Philadelphia upon the steamer
Republic." The route is by ferry from South Street to Gloucester, through West-
ille, Woodbury, Barnsboro, Pitman Grove, Glassboro, Franklinville, Malaga, Willow
rove, Vineland, Millville, Port Elizabeth, Bricksboro, Leesburg, Ewing's Creek,
.ast Creek, Dennisville, Goshen, Dias Creek, Rio Grande and Bennett to Cape May
ity. Total distance, eighty-five miles. While this little excursion involves some
and pounding and considerable inquiry, it is, in the main, a very pleasant tour.

BLACKWOODTOWN PIKE, N. J.

Many a cyclist, endeavoring to make his way out of Camden City toward the Haddonfield or the White Horse Pike, passes by the northern extremity of the Black woodtown Pike without noticing it or without dreaming that the nondescript sandy track on his right, east of the Starr's railroad crossing, is the beginning of a pike.

Starting from this very point, as Ephraim Avenue, alongside the railroad track which it crosses westward a short distance farther, it passes by Evergreen Cemetery and becomes a good wheelway beyond the first tollgate, past Northmont Lake (skaters, jot it in your notebook for next season) right on to Mount Ephraim and for a mile or two beyond it. As to the balance of it, through Runnemede and Chew' Landing, the best comment on its present condition may be expressed by a ferven hope that it may soon be the reverse of what it now is.

The distance from Camden Ferry to Blackwoodtown is twelve miles. The country is decidedly rolling for New Jersey.

HADDONFIELD PIKE.

The old-time Haddons would have no cause to be very proud either of Haddon Avenue, within Camden City, or of Haddonfield Pike outside of it should they re visit the scenes of their former life and judge of these thoroughfares according to ou modern standard of road construction.

A wretched pavement, which, were it offensive to the genuine article to designate as Belgian block, suggests the query as to whether any improvement has taken plac here ever since the time when our Continentals and British mercenaries tramped thi road to and fro during our Revolutionary struggle. Nor does the fitful assistance o an ill-trodden path make things appreciably better for the cyclist.

Although the centre of Haddonfield is not quite seven miles from Camden Ferry it is best reached at the cost of a little detour by way of the White Horse Pike, an the same applies to the only two intermediate localities along the Haddonfield Pike viz., Collingswood and Westmont. As to points south of Haddonfield, the Whit Horse Pike affords, beyond comparison, the easier access to them.

MARLTON PIKE, N. J.

The Marlton Pike is a continuation of State Street, Camden, eastward from Cooper Creek. On reaching the River Road it dips toward the southeast, crosse the Moorestown Pike at Stockton, and makes directly through Cooperstown, Ellis burg (where it meets the Haddonfield and Moorestown Road), and the hamlets of Ow Town and Locust Grove to Marlton, near the head waters of Pensauken Creek. It i a pike in the sense that the privilege of using it has to be paid for with a toll; and in truth, there are worse turnpikes, yet nothing like the comfort of the White Hors Pike or the Woodbury Pike should be looked for along its course. It affords, alon with the Moorestown Pike, the means of an out-and-home triangular trip of abou thirty miles; but the connecting link between Marlton and Moorestown is anythin but pleasant. The distance from Camden Ferry to Marlton is eleven miles.

MOORESTOWN ROAD, N. J.

Moorestown Road is the prolongation eastward of Federal Street, Camden After parting company with the Burlington Pike at Stockton it runs up and dow through Dudley and Rosedale to pretty Merchantville; thence through Maple Shad to Moorestown.

Like the Haddonfield Pike, this road is paved with so-called Belgian blocks. I has not worn quite so unevenly, perhaps, but it is far from an ideal wheelway. It frequent hills, too, accentuate its drawbacks more forcibly than is usually the cas with the average New Jersey flat road. The cyclist will find it to his advantage t avoid more than half its length by means of a triangular detour east of Merchant ville. Just outside the town let him branch off to the right down Church Roa until he reaches the Haddonfield and Moorestown Road, a distance of less than thre miles, and then follow the latter to his destination.

Beyond Moorestown lies Mount Holly, whose annual fair and bicycle meet ar too well known to require more than a mention here.

BURLINGTON PIKE.

The Burlington Pike might be described as the base of a very irregular triangl of which the River Road forms the other sides. From Stockton to Burlington it course is a practically straight line running through Morrisville, Cinnaminson, Fai view and Bridgeboro to its terminal point where Assiscunk Creek throws itself int the Delaware.

The sandy roadway is none of the best, and the path by its side proves a frien in need to the wheelman. He should not forget either that less than two hundre years ago this section was traveled through by none but Indians, and that this tim one hundred years ago geographers barely indicated this road as a track leadin hrough the wilderness from "Bridlington *vulgo* Burlington" to "Cooper's Ferry," ir present Camden.

The *Pennsylvania Chronicle* for March 23, 1767, is authority for the statement hat the distance was then reckoned "seventeen miles from Burlington Court-house the east end of Cooper's lane."

RIVER ROAD, N. J.

The River Road, as its name implies, skirts the river Delaware, and affords a lore or less desirable thoroughfare through the various waterside localities between amden and Burlington ; a delightful ride it would be on a hot summer's evening nder altered circumstances.

Its eastern extremity, from Cooper's Creek, through Pavonia to Beideman's and 'ish House, is so poor that the latter is generally reached by way of the Burlington ike. Beyond this point it is either cyclable or redeemed by a ridable path through 'elair, Palmyra and Riverton to Riverside. Here three miles of it have been piked, ie remainder of it, through Beverly and Edgewater Park, is good or improving.

The distance to Burlington by this River Road is about twenty miles.

Riverton, with its lively Athletic Association and its popular race track, de-·rves a special mention in connection with this road. Its meets are the Mecca of iany a cycling pilgrim during the racing season.

ELEVATIONS ABOVE TIDE WATER.

:ity Hall..	40 feet.
;ighteenth and Spring Garden Streets...	75 "
;road Street and Montgomery Avenue...	88 "
'ineteenth Street and Columbia Avenue..	107 "
'hirty-third and Diamond Streets....	108 "
·trawberry Mansion..	127 "
'wenty-second Street and Lehigh Avenue............	113 "
;road Street and Rising Sun Lane..................................,..............	100 "
'wenty-third and Venango Streets...	127 "
iixty-fifth Street and Woodland Avenue..	75 "
;altimore Avenue and Gray's Lane...	94 "
'orty-ninth Street and Chester Avenue..	84 "
.ancaster Avenue and Belmont Avenue..	105 "
iixty-first and Market Streets..	100 "
iixty-first Street and Haverford Road...	124 "
iixty-third Street, south of Lancaster Pike..	200 "
.ancaster Avenue and City Line...................................	226 "
:ity Line Road, at Bala..	260 "
:ity Line Road, at Belmont Avenue...	292 "
;elmont Avenue and Elm Avenue...	235 "
)xford Pike, at Olney...	112 "
Iill Street, Germantown, at Magnolia Avenue...	217 "
;reen and Carpenter Streets, Germantown........................,..............	232 "
;ermantown Road, at Mount Airy...	334 "
;ermantown Avenue, at Chestnut Hill...	433 "
;ummit Street, at Chestnut Hill..	440 "
)resheim Avenue and Cheltenham Avenue...	406 "
;idge Avenue, near Reservoir..	355 "
;idge Avenue, near City Line..	409 "
York Pike, at Olney Road..	203 "
York Pike, at Branchtown..	216 "
York Pike, at City Line...	233 "
)xford Pike, at Cottman Street..	137 "
)xford Pike, at Fox Chase...	209 "

INNS AND ROAD HOUSES.

FAIRMOUNT PARK.

East Side—Lemon Hill, Dairy at Mt. Pleasant, Strawberry Mansion, Tissot's, 'urf Villa, Riverside.

West Side—Belmont Mansion, Park Entrance Restaurant at Belmont Avenue, :hamounix.

Wissahickon—Maple Shade, Wissahickon Hall, Lotus Inn, Indian Rock, Valley ;reen, Wissahickon Inn.

MONTGOMERY PIKE.

Wisconsin House, General Wayne, Cyclers' Rest, Brockhurst Inn.

OLD YORK ROAD.

Restaurant at Logan Station, Clayton's at Branchtown, Du Bree's at Ogontz Beechwood at Jenkintown, Cottman House at Jenkintown, Mineral Spring at Willow Grove, Casino at Willow Grove.

BETHLEHEM PIKE.

" Wheel Water Pump " Hotel, Black Horse Hotel at Flourtown, Farmers' and Citizens' Hotel at Flourtown, Stahlnecker's at Flourtown, Fort-side Inn, Fort Washington, Ambler at Ambler Station, Wyndham at Ambler Station.

FRANKFORD ROAD.

Seven Stars at Frankford, Jolly Post at Frankford, Kiggin's at Frankford.

BRISTOL PIKE.

Green Tree at Holmesburg, General Wayne at Collegeville, Washington at Holmesburg, Red Lion at Torresdale, Morrelton Inn at Torresdale, United States at Trenton.

LANCASTER PIKE.

Red Lion at Ardmore, Evans' Rest at Bryn Mawr, Bryn Mawr at Bryn Mawr Devon Inn at Devon, Spread Eagle.

WOODLAND AVENUE.

Blue Bell at Paschalville, Buttonwood Inn at Darby.

CHESTER PIKE.

White Horse at Norwood, Ridley Park at Ridley Park, Cambridge House at Chester.

GERMANTOWN ROAD.

General Wayne, Mermaid Inn, Wyndmoor Hotel.

TINICUM ROAD.

Miller's at Essington, Griffin's at Essington.

GULF ROAD.

King of Prussia.

PENROSE FERRY ROAD.

Point Breeze Track House.

WHITE HORSE PIKE, N. J.

White Horse Inn, Laurel Springs Hotel.

BLACKWOODSTOWN PIKE.

Mt. Ephraim Hotel, Northmont Hotel, Jackson House.

BURLINGTON PIKE.

Bridgeboro Hotel, Belden at Burlington.

BUSTLETON PIKE.

Somerton Hotel.

OLD SECOND STREET PIKE.

Fox Chase Inn, Sorrel Horse, Yerkes', Bethayres, Lady Washington.

LIMEKILN PIKE.

Edge Hill, Fitzwatertown, Jarrettown, Three Tons.

PERKIOMEN PIKE.

Perkiomen Bridge Hotel, Fountain Inn at Barren Hill.

SKIPPACK PIKE.

Broad Axe, Blue Bell.

RIDGE PIKE.

Marple's, Black Horse, Farmers' at Norristown, Taylor's Hotel at Norristown, West End at Norristown.

WEST CHESTER ROAD.

Eagle at Manoa, Newtown Square Hotel.

BALTIMORE PIKE.

Cherry Tree at West Philadelphia, Strathaven Inn at Swarthmore, Charter House at Media, Clifton Heights Hotel.

PRINCIPAL CYCLING CLUBS IN AND NEAR PHILADELPHIA.

Americus Wheelmen, 2013 North Broad Street.
Centaur Bicycle Club, 2026 Rittenhouse Street.
Century Wheelmen, 1606 North Broad Street.
Columbia Cyclers, 1636 Diamond Street.
Century Wheelmen, Broad Street, above Oxford Street.
Eclipse Wheelmen, 4226 Brown Street.
Frankford Bicycle Club, 4640 Frankford Avenue.
Holmesburg Wheelmen, Holmesburg.
Ivy Wheelmen, 3227 Woodland Avenue.
Keystone Wheelmen, 1505 Moyamensing Avenue.
Liberty Wheelmen, 413 North Ninth Street.
Lulu Wheelmen, 1919 Franklin Street.
Medical and Pharmaceutical Bicycle Club, Sixteenth and Race Streets.
Meteor Wheelmen, 762 South Broad Street.
North East Wheelmen, 1856 Frankford Avenue.
Oxford Wheelmen, 2401 Oxford Street.
Pennsylvania Bicycle Club, 3940 Girard Avenue.
Philadelphia Bicycle Club, Twenty-sixth and Perot Streets.
Philadelphia Cycle and Field Club, Ardmore, Pa.
Penn Wheelmen, 2016 Diamond Street.
Philadelphia Wheelmen, 200 South Thirty-ninth Street.
Quaker City Wheelmen, 1402 Oxford Street.
South End Wheelmen, Broad and Morris Streets.
South West Cycle Club, 1706 Federal Street.
Time Wheelmen, 811 North Broad Street.
Kenilworth Wheelmen, 3859 Lancaster Avenue.
Loughran Bicycle Club, 120 East Chelten Avenue, Germantown.
St. Stephen's Wheelmen's Association, 5249 Wakefield Street, Germantown.
Castle Wheelmen, 1335 Castle Avenue.
Wisbet Athletic Club (Bicycle Branch), 1704 North Eighteenth Street.
Washington Square Wheelmen, 607 Pine Street.
Indiana Cycling Club, 3041 Lawrence Street.
Tioga Wheelmen, Mather and Venango Streets.
Clipper Wheelmen, Frankford.
Corsair Wheelmen, 2331 Dean Street.
Crescent Wheelmen, Camden.
Philadelphia Turner Cyclists, 435 North Sixth Street.
Vernon Cycle Club, Main and Harvey Streets, Germantown.
Wax End Wheelmen, Frankford and Oxford Streets, Frankford.
White Fawn Cycle Club, Mascher Street and Girard Avenue.
Young Men's Christian Association Wheelmen, Association Hall, Germantown.
Collingswood Wheelmen, Collingswood, N. J.
Clover Wheelmen, Bustleton.
Wayne Cycling Club, Lancaster Pike, Wayne.
Tacony Wheelmen, Tacony.
Brandywine Wheelmen, West Chester, Pa.
Chester Bicycle Club, Chester, Pa.
Stockton Wheelmen, Camden.
Wissahickon Wheelmen, Germantown Avenue, Germantown.
Owl Wheelmen, 1212 Columbia Avenue.
Roxborough Wheelmen, Ridge Avenue and Green Lane.
Diamond Wheelmen, 2117 Orthodox Street.
C. T. A. Wheelmen, 311 North Sixteenth Street.
Fairhill Hill Wheelmen, 2742 North Fifth Street.
West Side Wheelmen, 4119 Lancaster Avenue.
Acme Wheelmen, 338 South Twenty-second Street.
Clearfield Bicycle Club, 2953 Ruth Street, Kensington.
Forest Wheelmen, 4919 Girard Avenue.
Fried Oyster Cyclers, Wakefield and Jefferson Streets, Germantown.
Hygia Bicycle Club, 124 Diamond Street.
Tioga Cricket Club (Bicycle Branch).
Ho Bo Wheelmen, 1702 Venango Street.
Idle Hour Wheelmen.
Lehigh Wheelmen, Lehigh Avenue and Germantown Avenue.
Liberty Wheelmen, Ninth and Noble Streets.
Manheim Wheelmen, 5112 Wakefield Street.
Persimmon Cyclists, 2926 Ridge Avenue.
Pilot Wheelmen, 3137 Frankford Avenue.
Schuylkill Navy Wheelmen, 1626 Arch Street.
Silver Crown Bicycle Club, 2334 Ellsworth Street.
Silver Star Wheelmen, northwest corner Eleventh and Rodman Streets.
United States Military Wheelmen, 1520 North Thirteenth Street.
University of Pennsylvania Cycle Squad.
Philadelphia Field and Cycle Club, Ardmore.
Wissahickon Wheelmen, 431 Green Street, Germantown.

Philadelphia, Colonnade.
Burlington, Belden.
Bristol, Clossou's.
Willow Grove, Mineral Spring.
Woodbury, Paul's.
Vineland, Baker.
Millville, Doughty's.
Cape May, Congress Hall.
Swedesboro, Ford's.
Woodstown, Woodstown H.
Salem, Nelson.
Bridgeton, Cumberland.

Newtown, White Hall.
King of Prussia, K. of P. Inn.
Bryn Mawr, Evans' Rest, or B. M. Hot
Norristown, Farmers'.
Wilmington, Clayton House.
West Chester, Green Tree.
Media, Charter House.
Lansdowne, Junction.
Chester, Cambridge.
Paoli, Shoemaker's.
Devon, Devon Inn.
Phoenixville, Phoenix.

A "CENTURY" AND TWO FIFTY-MILE ROUTES WITHIN THE CITY LIMITS.

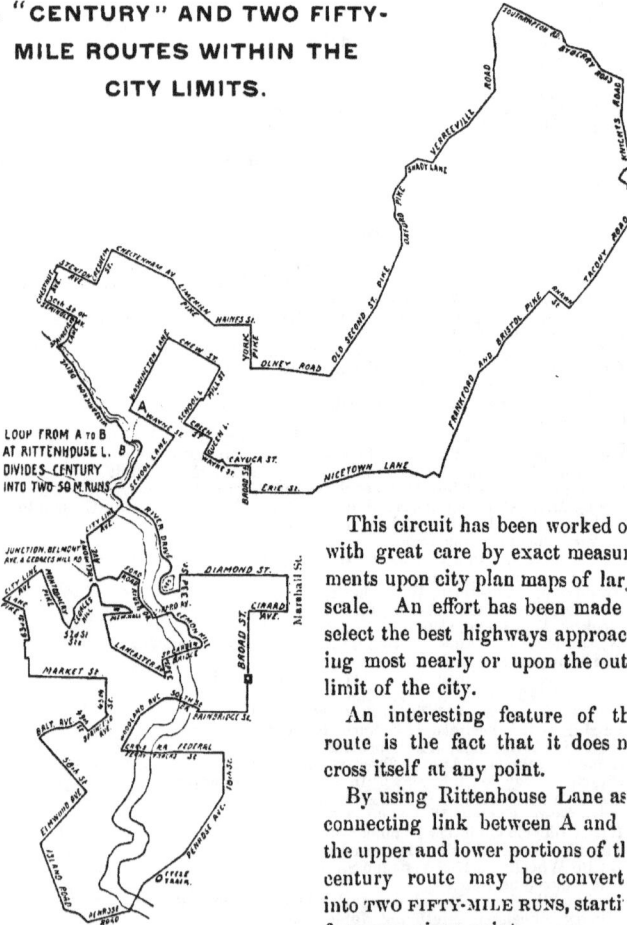

This circuit has been worked o with great care by exact measur ments upon city plan maps of lar scale. An effort has been made select the best highways approac ing most nearly or upon the out limit of the city.

An interesting feature of tl route is the fact that it does n cross itself at any point.

By using Rittenhouse Lane a connecting link between A and the upper and lower portions of tl century route may be convert into TWO FIFTY-MILE RUNS, starti from any given point.

The entire route, except the roads in the extreme northern portio takes the rider over excellent surfaces familiar to nearly all of t wheeling public.

34

The Fastest Wheel in the
World is the——➤

EASY RUNNING

$$\mathfrak{Syracuse}$$

Its Riders are Winners

PARK CYCLE CO.

916 Arch Street

PHILADELPHIA ...

Insist upon having

THE HITCHCOCK SPECIALTY CO.'S

Electrical

Take no
other ...

BICYCLE LUBRICATING
AND BURNING OILS

35

PENNSYLVANIA RAILROAD, SINGLE-TRIP FARES.

IN EFFECT MARCH 16, 1896.

Between Philadelphia and		Between Philadelphia and	
Allen Lane	$0 20	Media	$0
Audalusia	37	Merchantville	
Angora	12	Merion	
Ardmore	21	Moorestown	
Bala	15	Morton	
Berwyn	44	Mount Holly	
Beverly	39	Narberth	
Bonnaffou	12	Norristown	
Bordentown	70	Norwood	
Bridesburg	20	Overbrook	
Bristol	57	Palmyra	
Bryn Mawr	26	Paoli	
Burmont	18	Paschall	
Chadd's Ford	80	Phoenixville	
Chester Heights	58	Primos	
Chestnut Hill	20	Radnor	
Claymont, Del	47	Ridley Park	
Conshohocken	34	Riverside	
Crum Lynne	28	Riverton	
Cynwyd	15	Rosemont	
Darby	15	St. David's	
Delanco	33	Sharon Hill	
Devon	41	Shawmont	
Eddington	44	Swarthmore	
Eddystone	31	Tacony	
Fern Hill	73	Thurlow	
Fernwood	14	Torresdale	
Fifty-eighth Street	10	Trenton	
Forty-ninth Street	10	Tulpohocken	
Frankford	15	Upsal	
Germantown	13	Villa Nova	
Glen Mills	51	Wallingford	
Glen Riddle	42	Wawa	
Gloucester	10	Wayne	
Gray's Ferry	10	Wenonah	
Haddonfield	20	West Chester	
Haverford	23	Wilmington	
Holmesburg	28	Woodbury	
Kennett	1 01	Woodstown	
Lansdowne	16	Wynnewood	
Manayunk	15		

Charge for checking bicycles, 15 cents.

READING RAILROAD, SINGLE-TRIP FARES.

IN EFFECT MARCH 16, 1896.

Between Philadelphia and		Between Philadelphia and	
Allegheny Avenue, Pa	$0 05	Falls, Pa	$0
Ambler, Pa	41	Fern Rock, Pa	
Ashbourne, Pa	12	Fishers, Pa	
Atlantic City, N. J	1 25	Fort Washington, Pa	
Audubon, N. J	14	Frankford, Pa	
Barrington, N. J	18	Fulmor, Pa	
Bellevue, Pa	07	Garden Lake, Pa	
Bellmawr, N. J	18	Germantown, Pa	
Bell Road, Pa	16	Gibson's Point, Pa	
Blenheim, N. J	28	Glendora, N. J	
Blue Anchor, N. J	57	Glenside, Pa	
Bonair, Pa	33	Glen Willow, Pa	
Bridgeport, Pa	45	Gloucester, N. J	
Camp Hill, Pa	30	Gravers, Pa	
Chestnut Hill, Pa	15	Gwynedd, Pa	
Chew's Landing, N. J	25	Hammonton, N. J	
Clementon, N. J	32	Hathoro, Pa	
Columbia Avenue, Pa	05	Heaton, Pa	
Darby Creek, Pa	31	Hillside, Pa	
Eastwicks, Pa	07	Ivy Rock, Pa	
Eighty-fourth Street, Pa	17	Jenkintown, Pa	
Elmwood, Pa	18	King of Prussia, Pa	
Erie Avenue, Pa	06	Langhorne, Pa	
Essington, Pa	29	Lansdale, Pa	

(CONTINUED ON PAGE 38.)

Between Philadelphia and		Between Philadelphia and	
Lawnton, Pa..........................	$0 10	Port Kennedy, Pa.....................	$0 54
Logan, Pa..............................	07	Rosedale, N. J......................	67
Magnolia, N. J.......................	22	Rubicam, Pa.........................	19
Manayunk, Pa........................	12	School Lane, Pa.....................	10
Melrose, Pa...........................	10	Sellersville, Pa....................	1 02
Merion, Pa............................	51	Shawmont, Pa.......................	20
Mill Road, Pa........................	40	Somerton, Pa.......................	41
Mount Airy, Pa......................	12	Spring Mill, Pa....................	31
Mount Ephraim, N. J...............	15	Tioga, Pa...........................	05
Neshaminy Falls, Pa...............	53	Traymore, Pa.......................	46
New Britain, Pa.....................	96	Trevose, Pa........................	47
Nicetown, Pa.........................	05	Twenty-second Street, Pa..........	05
Ninety-second Street, Pa.........	19	Valley Forge, Pa...................	58
Norristown, Pa......................	45	Walnut Lane, Pa....................	10
North Essington, Pa................	24	Wayne Junction, Pa................	07
Oaklyn, N. J.........................	12	West Collingswood, N. J...........	10
Oak Lane, Pa.........................	10	West Conshohocken, Pa.............	34
Ogontz, Pa............................	12	West Manayunk, Pa.................	12
Penbryn, N. J........................	42	West Spring Mill, Pa..............	31
Penllyn, Pa..........................	47	White Horse, Pa....................	66
Pennbrook, Pa........................	69	White Marsh, Pa....................	60
Pennington, N. J....................	1 05	Wingohocking, Pa...................	10
Perkiomen Junction, Pa............	62	Wissahickon, Pa....................	10
Phoenixville, Pa....................	70	Woodland, N. J.....................	82
Pomona, N. J.........................	1 00	Yardley, Pa........................	80

BALTIMORE AND OHIO RAILROAD, SINGLE-TRIP FARES.

IN EFFECT MARCH 16, 1896.

Between Philadelphia and		Between Philadelphia and	
East Side..............................	$0 05	Fairview............................	$0 28
P. & R. Junction....................	06	Chester.............................	32
Bartram..............................	06	Upland..............................	32
Sixtieth Street......................	08	Felton..............................	38
Mount Moriah........................	09	Twin Oaks...........................	42
Seventieth Street...................	10	Boothwyn............................	41
Darby................................	12	Ogden...............................	46
Boone................................	13	Carpenter...........................	49
Collingdale..........................	15	Harvey..............................	52
Oakeola..............................	17	Silver Side.........................	54
Llanwellyn...........................	17	Carrcroft...........................	57
Holmes...............................	20	Concord.............................	63
Folsom...............................	22	Augustine...........................	64
Ridley...............................	24	Wilmington..........................	67
Milmont..............................	25		

Bicycles are carried free of charge, owner's risk.

39

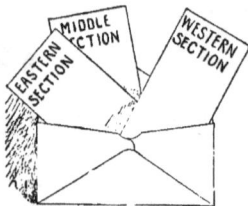

ARE YOU A MEMBER OF THE

...L. A. W.?

A FEW REASONS FOR JOINING

BECAUSE a membership means privileges which can be secured in no other way, and which will repay many times over, the nominal cost involved.

Because it is the only "square" thing to do. Any rider who is not a member of the League of American Wheelmen is enjoying privileges which others are paying for.

A handsome leather-bound road-book (obtainable nowhere else at any price) is given to every member. This book, prepared by the gratuitous labor of Pennsylvania League members, gives over 200 cycling routes in Pennsylvania and vicinity, as well as many favorite through tours in other sections of the country. It gives the distances between towns, tells the condition, material and grade of every road traversed, names a hotel in nearly every town at which special rates will be given to L. A. W. members, and gives much other valuable information.

A new and revised road-map of the State on an enlarged scale, printed on bond paper and published for convenience in three sections, is also sent to every member.

THE L. A. W. BULLETIN AND GOOD ROADS is the weekly official organ of the League. The amount named below includes a year's subscription. It contains all the current cycling news, interesting descriptive matter relating to tours, tells how wheels should be cared for, and supplies unlimited practical information to the inquiring cyclist.

Every member is *guaranteed* full legal protection (without cost) in case of infringement of his or her rights as a cyclist on the road, on railroads or elsewhere. The Pennsylvania Division of the L. A. W. has *never lost a single case* of this kind in the courts.

In nearly every town is a local officer, called a Consul. Your membership card is an introduction to this official, who will give you any reasonable assistance.

The League of American Wheelmen is the pioneer organization in the movement for better roads. It has spent over $100,000 in this cause alone. It requires numbers and influence to push this movement, as well as to defeat legislation intended to curtail the rights of wheelmen, secure concessions from railroads in the way of free transportation for bicycles and further the many other objects in which all riders are interested.

It controls absolutely all bicycle racing in this country.

It costs but $2.00 for the first year and $1.00 for each succeeding year to entitle you to all the privileges of membership.

If any further information is wanted address the

PENNSYLVANIA DIVISION SECRETARY

Box 1177, PHILADELPHIA

The **Pocket** $5.00
─. **Kodak**

A practical camera for the cyclist. So small that it can be slipped into the pocket or carried in a case that's no larger than a tool bag . . ,

The Pocket Kodak Bicycle Carrying Case containing camera and 3 extra spools of film.

"ONE BUTTON DOES IT YOU PRESS IT"

Pocket Kodak, loaded for 12 pictures 1½ x 2 in., $5.00.
Developing and Printing Outfit, - - $1.50

Eastman Kodak Co.
ROCHESTER, N. Y.

Sample photo and booklet for two 2-cent stamps.

THE COLUMBIA STANDARD BICYCLE OF THE WORLD

GRACEFUL, light and strong, this product of the oldest bicycle establishment in America still retains its place at the head. Always well up to the times or a little in advance, its well deserved and ever increasing popularity is a source of pride and gratification to its makers. To ride a bicycle and not to ride a Columbia is to fall short of the fullest enjoyment of a noble sport.

$100 BUYS ANY PATTERN.
Art Catalogue, describing the entire line, mailed on request.

HART CYCLE CO., PIONEER CYCLE HOUSE,
816 ARCH STREET, PHILADELPHIA.

41

WHAT THE L. A. W. OFFICIALS SAY ABOUT "BEST ROUTES."

OFFICE OF SAMUEL A. BOYLE, CHIEF CONSUL PENNA. DIVISION, No. 654
CITY HALL, PHILADELPHIA.

PHILADELPHIA, 12 March, 1896.

Mr. Frank H. Taylor, Philadelphia.

DEAR SIR:—After hearing of your pamphlet detailing the features of the roads surrounding Philadelphia, I have no hesitation in saying that I believe it will meet with a favorable reception on the part of the bicyclers of Philadelphia, and that it will prove to be a valuable supplement to the road book of the Pennsylvania Division of the League of American Wheelmen.

Yours truly,

S. A. BOYLE, *Chief Consul.*

OFFICE CHAIRMAN OF RACING BOARD, L. A. W.

March 14, 1896.

Mr. Frank H. Taylor, Philadelphia.

DEAR SIR:—I have inspected the advance sheets of your book, "Best Routes in and around Philadelphia," and am immensely pleased with its scope and the maps provided.

Very truly yours,

GEO. D. GIDEON.

PHILADELPHIA, March 16, 1896.

I have carefully examined Mr. Frank H. Taylor's book, "Best Routes for Wheelmen," and feel sure that any rider who sees it will bear me out in saying that it is the best guide in its line (*i. e.,* for local riding) which has ever been published.

It contains much valuable information about our historic landmarks not generally known to the bulk of our riders.

For those of our wheelmen (and they are many) who care only for short rides, this book will prove of the greatest service, and worth many times the small price charged for it. The maps are not only clear and well engraved, but what is more to the point, they are *accurate.*

W. W. RANDALL,
Chairman Penna. Road Book Comm.

43

Index.

www.ingramcontent.com/pod-product-compliance
Lightning Source LLC
Chambersburg PA
CBHW021643270326
41931CB00008B/1139